WELSH CRAFTS

Robert Griffiths, Blacksmith working at Llechwedd Slate Mine

Mary Eirwen Jones

WELSH CRAFTS

*An account of the historic Welsh crafts
and as they exist today*

B. T. Batsford Ltd, London

First published 1978
© Mary Eirwen Jones 1978

Printed in Great Britain by
The Anchor Press Ltd, Tiptree, Essex
for the publishers B. T. Batsford Ltd,
4 Fitzhardinge Street, London W1H 0AH
Bound by Wm Brendon & Son Ltd, Tiptree, Essex

ISBN 0 7134 1087 6

Contents

Illustrations

Acknowledgements

The author and publishers would like to thank the following for their permission to reproduce the illustrations in this book: Ammonite Ltd no. 27; British Legion Factory, Llanwrtyd no. 2; the Abbot, Caldey no. 24; Craft Centre Cymru no. 3; Folk Museum of Wales, St Fagans no. 10; Hywel Davies no. 11; H. Edwards no. 9; *Evening Telegraph*, Coventry no. 25; Harlech Television no. 1; National Museum of Wales nos 21, 22; Newton Sealey no. 15; Taurus Pottery no. 20; R. Thomas no. 18; Tregaron Craft Centre no. 19; Welsh Tourist Board nos 13, 23, 26; M. Wight nos 6, 7, 8, 12, 17; P. Wilson no. 16; *Y Cymro* no 14.

'Is there a gatekeeper?' asked Culwch.
'Yes, and if you do not keep silence you will be beheaded.'
'Open the gate!'
'I will not open it!'
'What is the reason that you will not open it?'
'The knife is in the food, drink is in the horn and there is rejoicing in the hall; and no one shall enter the Court of Arthur unless he is a King of a free country, or a craftsman plying a craft.'

These words from the *Mabinogion*, the collection of legendary Welsh tales, show that crafts have had from early times a strong cultural significance in Wales. Much that is best in Welsh culture derives from craftsmanship.

Preface

A strong resurgence of interest is evident today in the crafts in Wales. The tradition of craftsmanship in the country is very old. Like the hills and castles, it was for a long time taken for granted; it was associated with a distant past; it was regarded as being relatively unimportant, as having no direct relevance with a later age.

Now, however, crafts are subjects of foremost interest. Their functional, economic, aesthetic and also their therapeutic worth is being more justly assessed.

Increasing numbers of people are devoting themselves to the crafts. Many who practise them live in the rural areas of Wales where the crafts have their natural setting. Many people who are accustomed to urban ways of life, are, in this more ethnic age, attracted to the crafts.

Craftsmanship is a wide subject. What is a craft? Ideally, it is accepted as being the skill of one, who, by training and tradition, undertakes certain specific work wherein, by hand, he carries through all the stages of that work himself. He and the job are one. Moreover, he works for an individual; he knows his customer and his special needs; he is there to answer for his product, and therefore aims at efficiency and sound workmanship. He makes use of local materials and subscribes to local needs. Traditionally, all this is true. But such a definition of a craftsman and his work have passed away in some measure, giving place to standards demanded by a Machine Age, which has, as its basis, a society demanding mass production, and which is keenly competitive and commercially conscious.

Where does craft end, and where does art begin? What exactly is an artist-craftsman? Does craftsmanship involve the finished product, or has it a bearing on social status? Then, what of the standards of craftsmanship? The premise that an article is hand-made does not ensure that it is of sound craftsmanship, nor that it is beautiful. What is a craft, and what is an industry? Are they opposed to each other, are they inter-related, or do their spheres in the present age over-lap? The deeper one ponders on these questions, the greater their number seems to grow.

The polemics of definition and of standards cannot be evolved universally. Fortunately, there are thousands who seek no precise or academic answers. There are people who can enter into the joy of creation and who can share in the mellow philosophy of a true craftsman, seeing in his work, 'a thing of beauty, and a joy forever'.

Wales is particularly fortunate in having the Welsh Folk Museum at Cardiff. It is unique. Full credit must be given to the knowledge, foresight and organising ability of those who established it, and who, later, developed it. Just value has here been given to craftsmanship in Wales, as it was in the past, and as it is practised today.

The Wales Tourist Board has done much to help visitors. Among other things, it has published a small but very helpful book – *Wales; Crafts and Rural Industries*. This gives clear information concerning craft-work shops; routes, places, times of visiting and other relevent data. The foreword contains a tribute to the craftsmen and women in Wales:

'The craftworker has always held a valued and respected place in the community, and the isolation of many rural villages gave rise to many country crafts. This loneliness and isolation is one of the reasons why many of the younger artists and crafts workers have settled in these communities, to create amongst the hills of Wales objects of beauty and self-expression from natural materials.

'It is difficult to separate the concepts of art and craft. Craft products in early days were produced to serve a specific need and function; today, artistic individuality forms an important part in their production.

'The craftsman's flair, skill and intimate knowledge of the basic material raise many products to an art form. In many of the items which the visitor can see and buy, the material used is indigenous – slate, wood, stone, clay, leather and metal – and the individual craftworker and artist combines imagination and ideas with basic skill, so that each object has a special quality and individuality which the visitor can see and enjoy for himself.'

Individuality is indeed a main element in craftsmanship, and it must of necessity permeate any treatment of the subject. Selection in this book among the many forms practised has been an unavoidable but sad necessity.

It would be foolish to approach the subject with romantic but unseeing eyes. One faces the fact that many who have come to live in Wales for the purpose of practising their craft are baffled by the economics of their occupation, and find themselves immersed in an alien environment. Without the ability to persevere and to adapt themselves, they become disillusioned. There is deeper understanding for those idealists who find that the ever-widening net of craftsmanship is as yet not extensive enough to hold them; their purposes, the exigencies of their techniques, their standards prove contrary and unacceptable; sadly for themselves and for others they return from whence they came.

This book aims at giving information concerning Welsh Crafts as practised today, and also their tradition, for this continues as a living force and there are those who seek the revival of many crafts no longer practised. No strict boundaries of craftsmanship are observed. The field is a wide one and includes crafts-in-industry, such as those of fine porcelain and also japanned ware, for to many connoisseurs and collectors, this is the real connotation of Crafts in Wales.

A book, like a human being, depends on others for its creation and its sustenance. A heartfelt and very sincere tribute is given here to all those who have in rich goodwill, contributed to *Welsh Crafts*. May the help and happiness which they have so richly bestowed, rebound greatly and graciously to their good, and to that of our country.

Introduction

THE BUTTERMAKER

ANNIE DAVIES, Y LLAETHFERCH

Crafts in Wales have a long tradition. They are characterised by a virility derived from their functionalism. The real value of a craft was to create something *useful*; decoration was secondary. Through the centuries, craftsmanship, to a Welshman, has been an end in itself.

Crafts came into being early in civilised life. The early Celt, mastering his environment, shaped and refined materials to his greater use. As the elements became his servants, he hardened clay, he cut and polished stones, he used timber from the forests for building and for the construction of boats. He made weapons and improved them. When pride of possession entered into his mind, he delighted in ornamenting what he had made. His brain grew more alert, and he sensed, in ever-growing degree, the beauty of nature around him. His will to create was quickened. He reached out into the realm of art, creating crude images of himself, of his fellow men and, later, of deities, super-natural. In time he co-operated with his fellow craftsmen in building a house for himself, and then a temple for his God. As civilisation advanced with the centuries, craftsmanship continued to bind together the essential interests of human life. Men built houses which were more comfortable, and these were filled with furniture made by craftsmen.

The development and healthy growth of the mediaeval cities and towns derived their strength from the guilds of craftsmen. Every vocation was linked, directly or indirectly, with the craft workshops. The strength of these guilds varied considerably, but, officially and unofficially, their influence was far-reaching. During the Middle Ages, and during the succeeding centuries, Welshmen, in common with people of other European nations, were closely interested in craftsmanship. When united with other men in a guild, the craftsman yet remained an individual; his skill lay in the artistry and foresight of his own mind, and in the dexterity of his own hands.

The Renaissance led to a growth of Humanism. There grew up a strong, if subconscious, trend of thought, which was inclined to despise the old type of craftsmanship and which, in ever-growing degree, refused to see in the craftsmen of the time an aristocracy of labour. Craftsmen, however, continued to flourish. They achieved high standards of work. They fostered a national manifestation of craftsmanship, somewhat difficult to define, but unmistakably present. Much of their work was made to last; it served its own purpose, and also served as an inspiration for future craftsmen.

Craftsmanship in Wales derives much of its virility from the circumstance of situation. Soil and climate are always powerful determining influences. Craftsmanship was above all *purposive*. The craftsman co-operated actively with the husbandman in his battle against the elements. The Welshman was far removed from the peasant of Southern France or of Northern Italy, where Nature came more than half way to his assistance.

In the Middle Ages, Wales was essentially a land of peasants. There were but few rich patrons to encourage any but the minor arts. Consequently, craftsmanship, simple but essential, was given freedom to grow unhampered. National vicissitudes and influences of religion had their repercussions on development. The craftsmen had to consider the recipients of their work. They did not, however, only provide beautiful things; by precept and example, they felt obliged to cultivate the public taste. Invariably, the craftsmen of Wales were concerned with function; the products of their hands were there to serve a specific need. The use for which an article was intended determined its form. The beauty attained was often unconscious, and seldom drew attention to itself.

In her comparative isolation, Wales was in many ways able to develop and to maintain forms of craftsmanship which were individual. Social life in Wales was economically poor and politically turbulent. These forces helped to prevent mere blind imitation. When existent, imitative factors were often blunted by the time they reached Wales. When there was imitation, there was a time lag, of varying duration but nevertheless present. As a general estimate, a fashion or form which prevailed in England, or on the European continent, would become the vogue in the Principality a century or more late. Such a time lag may emphasise the isolation of Wales, her poverty and her poor communications; yet these also throw into relief the skill, the ingenuity and the hardihood of her native craftsmen. Traditions of style and technique prevailed.

The local tradition was given a local impress by the geographical character of Wales. Moreover, one of the prime purposes of the craftsman was – and still is – to serve a local and essential need. Often he has to seek his raw materials from close at hand. It was only with the advent of the Industrial Age that communications between North and South Wales, and, indeed, between East and West Wales, became reasonably easy. The absence of large towns had militated against commercial contacts. Chains of mountains and great central moorlands emphasised the isolation of localities. It was in such an environment that Welsh craftsmen had been able to thrive.

The influences of geographical and cultural habitat prevail today. The observations of the Keeper of the Department of Material Culture at the Welsh Folk Museum, St Fagans, Cardiff, are trenchant and cryptic:

'The age-old isolation, the lack of facilities for formal social events, and the long hours of solitude associated with a pastoral life have also had a profound effect on material culture. This is expressed in the products of craftsmanship and in the tools and equipment of the farm and the home. Much of Wales consists of inhospitable moorland with narrow valleys leading from the central core of upland like the spokes of a giant wheel. Much of the land is more than a thousand feet above the sea level, and in many parts is poor and stony while the climate is damp. Even in the more favoured valleys it is difficult for a farmer to take advantage of the natural condition of the soil if the rain pours down continuously. To obtain a good crop of barley or wheat, sunshine is essential, but when there are mists and rain, the farmer must adapt his agriculture to climatic conditions. No part of Wales may be said to be perfectly suited to the growth of cereal crops and, by tradition, Welsh society is a pastoral one; the keynote to its development has been animal husbandry rather than cereal cultivation. Sheep and cattle provided the raw materials for two important industries, those of woollen manu- facturing and leather production. Furthermore, livestock farming never needed the elaborate equipment of arable farming, and for this reason specialised craftsmen such as ploughwrights, schythe- handle and rake makers and wattle-hurdle weavers, so com- mon in English villages, were a rarity in Wales. All woodwork was carried out by country craftsmen who were able to construct everything in wood from fences to farm vehicles, and from coffins to tool handles; metal work was the province of the general blacksmith and not of specialised families of plough- wrights and scythe smiths and, as in peasant societies the world over, a great deal of the equipment of farm and home was made by the farmers themselves, rather than by craftsmen. In an up- land district of dispersed family small-holdings, the making of such things as farm gates, seedlips, baskets, tool handles, rakes and tools was also part of the routine of farming. Farmers often showed considerable artistry in their work, and the tradition of the amateur, the tradition of the part-timer, has given us perhaps the greatest expression of our material culture. We can imagine the life of no more than sixty years ago as being more leisurely than it is today. Entertainment was at a premium and most of the inhabitants practised some form of craft in their spare time. The things they produced were the utilitarian necessities of the farm and home, but as time progressed the product became purely decorative. It was this tradition that gave Wales its love spoons,

W.C.—B

its stay busks, knitting needle sheaths and basketry, products of an upland peasantry that lived in isolation.'*

Largely because of the isolation of localities, Welsh craftsmen had been able to survive until mass-produced, factory-made goods were brought into Wales. From the beginning of the Industrial Revolution, however, the number of craftsmen began to diminish. With the turn of the century, it became a tendency to regard the crafts as a dying form of creative expression, and to look upon those crafts that had managed to survive as the residue of a peasant economy.

With the advancing decades of this century there came a surge in public interest and an increase in the number of craftsmen. In all periods of history craftsmen have numbered few in the community. They are essentially the *contrivers*, the rest are recipients of their work.

No definite dates can be fixed as to the revival in craftsmanship, but it corresponds in general with the development of British agriculture. Crafts essentially play a powerful role in the natural economy. Rural craftsmen, in particular, are essential to the farmer. Large-scale farming and scientific agricultural methods are still affected by local conditions. It is the village craftsman with an intuitive and inherent knowledge of local needs and of usable raw materials to hand, who can most ably fill the farmer's specific needs.

The large-scale building programme of post-war years presupposes the co-operation of considerable bands of craftsmen, versatile in their skills. The educationist recognises, with ever-greater understanding, the worth of craftsmanship. He sees in the development of the skills something essential to the human race; something which fulfils a need which intricate machinery and mass ways of life can never fulfil.

In 1921 the Rural Industries Bureau was set up by the Ministry of Agriculture, at a time of severe agricultural depression, to aid small crafts. The record of the R.I.B. was a particularly worthy one. Through county organisers and instructors, it carried out activities on a wide scale, reaching to all villages and hamlets in Wales. By nature craftsmen are conservative, but the R.I.B. was able to bring about a gradual, but much needed, evolution.

*J. Geraint Jenkins, *Life and Tradition in Rural Wales*, London, J. M. Dent & Sons Ltd., 1976.

Today, help is given to craftsmen in various ways by several organisations. Some of them are government-sponsored; some represent the forward-looking policies of advanced craftsmen and artists. The Council for Small Industries in Rural Areas (C.O.S.I.R.A.), now taken over by the Welsh Development Agency, offers free scientific and technical advice; advisors and instructors visit the craftsmen, and help to solve problems peculiar to the person and place. Help and advice are given to younger craftsmen to establish themselves; of particular value is a most essential service of organising training and apprenticeship courses. All these contribute to a continuity of craftsmanship. The Welsh Folk Museum gives continuous help, guidance and inspiration. The Welsh Weavers Association Ltd has injected rich new life into the woollen industry of Wales, giving it what is fast becoming world-wide recognition. Other acknowledged bodies such as the Crafts Advisory Committee, The Design Centre, Craftcentre Wales, The Guild of Potters of North Wales and of South Wales, The Guild of Goldsmiths and Silversmiths of Wales, the Lace Society, Wales, and the Wales Tourist Board have contributed greatly, and continue to contribute, to the growth and increased status of crafts in Wales. Artist-craftsmen are encouraged to compete and to exhibit their work in Young Farmers' Clubs, in the Royal Welsh Agricultural Show and at the Royal National Eisteddfod of Wales.

Due to the stimulus of these and similar organisations, and largely due to individual initiative, the craftsman of today has the assurance that he is not faced with the problem of the mere survival of some small hereditary craft: on the contrary, he becomes aware of its rich potential; he is also aware of the value of the craft to the community in which he serves.

Even a casual observer can see that a marked change has been introduced into the workshops of the craftsmen themselves. These are, by tradition, scenes of orderly disorder. There, within a building often primitive, tables, benches and chairs are scarred with the toil of more than one generation. Work in process of being made appears alongside work that has been completed. Tools of all kinds, from the primitive to the intricate, lie around, festooned on the walls and on the door; and on the window ledges are the minutiae of the particular craft – chisels, hanks of wool, wire, pieces of leather, brads, hooks, needles and string.

Into these workshops, the advisors and technicians of the craft

organisations have introduced order. Welsh craftsmen have shown
themselves, at first willing, and later, eager, to avail themselves of
these professional services. On their part the organisations have
helped the craftsmen to maintain their own individuality. Thus a
happy *entente cordiale* exists. Much of the success of this relation-
ship lies in the fact that the official organisations do not look on
the crafts with sentimental eyes. The organisers recognise, along
with the craftsmen, that the craft is practised primarily for making
a living. Due value is, however, given to the aesthetic worth of the
craft; opportunities for encouraging pride in workmanship are
fostered. Care is bestowed on beauty of form, and in addition,
there is psychological encouragement, understanding and sympathy
towards the solitary worker. Most experienced craftsmen are now
recognised and acclaimed.

The solitariness of the craftsman of the past tended to support
the belief that craftsmanship was on the decline. Now, there is a
marked increase both in the numbers of people who practise various
crafts, and also in those who seek out those things which individual
craftsmen create, and in those who delight in seeing them made.
The Wales Tourist Board has done much to foster such interest. It
has recognised that the solitary craftsman has a magnetic appeal to
those living in densely populated areas. Visitors like to explore the
market towns of the North, and of the South, and, too, of Mid-
Wales, and the Border. Their pilgrimages bring them to places
where the crafts are practised, and to places where the older crafts
survive.

At the present time the crafts have shed their romantic associa-
tions. Utilitarianism makes a surer foundation. For example, property developers, among others, are well aware of it. As more than
one aesthetically-minded speculator has discovered, it is possible
to re-build an old Welsh house or *bwthyn*, and to enlist the services
of a local carpenter, smith and thatcher. The accessories of good
country living can still be supplied artistically by local turners,
potters, cloggers, basket-makers and textile weavers. There still
exists a discriminating public which prefers goods which are
not mass-produced. Granted a continuous and progressive need
for their products the future of such craftsmen is reasonably
assured.

The present age is one of specialisation. The craftsman, on the
contrary, has always prided himself on his versatility; there has

always been a diversity of skill, and a diversity of work. Aptly did Adam Smith write in his *Wealth of Nations* (1776):

> 'A country carpenter deals in every sort of work that is made of wood; a country smith in every sort of work that is made of iron. The former is not only a carpenter, but a joiner, a cabinet-maker, and even a carver in wood, as well as a wheelwright, a plough-wright, a cart and wagon builder.'

The words are, in principle, true today.

The craftsman is, in the main, a solitary worker. He has the ability – an ability which has grown increasingly uncommon – to work alone. His character gains strength from his solitariness, and from his pre-occupation with creative work. Craftsmen derive satisfaction from creative work, especially when they undertake all the processes of their craft. A natural balance and equipoise rank among the natural dividends. In proportion to the craftsman's effort to achieve perfection, is his joy in his own workmanship. The meta-physical aspect of craftsmanship must therefore have a special meaning to the modern world.

He may work in isolation, but the craftsman is fully aware of the need for a community when it comes to selling his wares. The Welsh Craft Fair held annually in Wales is proving a momentous success. It is sponsored by the Welsh Weavers' Association Ltd, and is supported by the Welsh Craft Association, the Small Pot-teries Trade Association, the Goldsmiths and Silversmiths Guild of Wales and the Welsh Garment Manufacturers Association. When the Fair is held, in the autumn, Llandrindod Wells becomes a national and international focus point. The enterprise has grown in steady arithmetical progression. There are now approximately two hundred contributors, and orders are estimated in several million pounds. Buyers congregate around the trade stands from all parts of the world. The organisers envisage acting collectively in the future. They hope to participate in a published index of rural work-shops, overseas missions organised by the Department of Trade, and the establishment of a regular display centre, and the issue of craft publications. Conscious of the wide market for Welsh crafts in tourism, the organisers of the Welsh Trade Fair hope to foster expert sales staff for export trade. The small one-man craft establishments in particular will find such projects helpful. Currently, one third of the companies exhibiting at the fair are small; a third are one-man establishments. A second third may employ up to fifty people. In the remainder, the number of employees ranges from fifty to two hundred.

Thus, all the workshops are relatively small. However, they are contributing substantially to the total economy of Wales. Mr. Dennis Clive, Managing Secretary of the Welsh Weavers Association, stated (1977):

> 'The craft industry is growing rapidly in Wales. We estimate that it has created 1,500 new jobs in rural areas in the past decade.'

He sees in the Welsh Craft Fair a turning point in the campaign to get wider markets for Welsh-made goods, and he sees in it the beginning of a movement which will introduce a wholly new approach for marketing for rural industry.

Thus the small craft workshops are becoming steadily big business in Wales and have potential for much future good. Commercially secure, the Welsh craftsman now continues to ply his craft, and while doing so, he balances his values and ponders over the ancient Welsh saying – '*Gwell crefft na golud*' – Better a craft than wealth – and concludes that he is happily content with the rewards of both.

I

Craft Centres

THE MILLER

DOUGLAS W. LICKLEY, Y MELINYDD

'Art needs commerce more than commerce needs art' is an established dictum. The craftsman needs a steady market for his goods. He needs a centre where the public will see his goods and buy them.

Invaluable work is being done by various craft centres, many of widely differing types, which are now established throughout Wales. Reference is made in this work to a selection of them. A book, *Craft Workshops in the Countryside*, published by C.O.S.I.R.A., has a clear, concise and very informative list of these. Details are given of the craft, its location, times of accessibility, export potential, and whether the type of craftwork is available for wholesale orders and commissioned work. The book also gives a comprehensive list of retail workshops in various areas.

The Craft Design Centre at Tregaron – Canolfan Cynllun Crefft Cymru – Dyfed, has justified its existence as a centre where the craftwork exhibited is guaranteed as *having been made by individual craftsmen in Wales*.

This is particularly in evidence in the pottery which is a prominent feature of the centre. None of the pottery displayed is made by mechanical methods of moulding, whereby but little skill is employed. Potters, who use the traditional methods of making clays and glazes from local soils, exhibit their work. They use wood-fired kilns. Considerable time is spent in preparing small sticks of wood for the firing. The individual potter sits for many hours at his kiln, controlling it with a practised eye. The price of work made with such care is of necessity higher than that produced by more mechanical methods, but the final product is well worth-while.

The Craft Centre at Tregaron has established the fact that there is now a substantial demand for work of a high standard. Such economic advance and also encouragement to workers, has brought rich reward to craftworkers.

This centre in Dyfed was established in 1971. It already has an international reputation for its high standards. Within Britain, too, it has considerable influence, and its efforts in raising the standards of craftsmanship in Wales, are acknowledged. It has encouraged the production of such things as barometers with Welsh signs on them; likewise, Welsh-language toys and educational projects, and colourful banners with Welsh lullabies printed on them.

A subsidiary yet, nevertheless, a very valuable part of the work of the centre is the promotion of small craftworkers who are endeavouring to earn a living in Wales. This helps to ensure the survival of some of the traditional country crafts of the Principality.

There is much variation in the goods displayed at the centre. Careful selection and personal inspection of craftsmen at their work, have resulted in an improvement in skills and in design. The number of craftsmen who recognise the worth of the centre and who are eager to participate, increases every year.

The organisers are ever-conscious of the fact that a craftsman usually produces better work when working on unique objects, than when supplying repetitive orders. Therefore, as far as is possible, they give craftworkers freedom wherein to express their own skill and style. In this way the work displayed is never standardised.

The economics of craftwork are always given careful assessment. Sympathetic hearing is given when the craftsmen come with their traditional complaint, that their best work is too costly, that it is not economically viable, that it is virtually impossible to sell it. A craftsman must of necessity receive a fair reward for his work. He is ill-advised if he goes on creating expensive work with no prospect of a sound return. The Tregaron centre fulfils an essential need by ensuring a market at a fair price.

Pottery holds a prominent position at the centre, but crafts of many kinds are shown. Work is displayed in stone, in wood and in iron, in skins, precious stones and other media. As is natural in *Canolfan Cynllun Crefft Cymru*, special emphasis is placed on traditional Welsh material and methods. The visitor might see a comprehensive collection of traditional wood-pegged furniture in oak, elm, ash, pine, etc., and also wooden tables and kitchenware. Recognising that slate is one of the best known raw materials of Wales, and also that its worth and possibilities are under-estimated, a number of products in this material is given prominence. The visitor can often see work that is exclusive and of a special nature. This is because the centre makes a speciality of *individual orders*, whereby craftsmen receive special commissions.

The Mid-Wales Gallery at Newbridge-on-Wye, Powys, is a highly selective gallery. It was started by Nancy Palmer Jones in 1972. Its influence has been considerable, not only in the world of art and of craftsmanship, but also in its rôle of making known the amenities of Central Wales to a wider world. It is both an Art Gallery and a Craft Shop. It has in the past – and it also continues – to bring together those artists who reside in the area. It has succeeded in uniting racial and ethnic qualities in natives and settlers. These now form a group which is particularly active and which claims that, in talent, originality and range, they rival any London-based group.

In the sphere of crafts, the gallery has constantly emphasised aesthetic values. A high standard of workmanship characterises all articles made by local craftsmen. Materials and designs must likewise be of a high standard. Craftwork displayed covers a wide range – jewellery, patchwork, candles, pottery, toys, woodwork, leatherwork. Many of the articles for sale are exclusive to the Mid-Wales house. Crafts practised at the gallery include toy-making, rug weaving, leatherwork. A speciality of the Mid-Wales house is the production of crocheted garments made from vegetable dyed wools.

Leaves and berries growing wild in the hills and valleys of Wales are collected. These are especially prepared by traditional methods, and are used to dye natural Welsh wool. The wool is then made up into jackets and jerseys in subtle colours, and in designs which are both unusual and elegant. They are much in demand, and through them the Mid-Wales house is becoming internationally known.

The Tegfryn Art Gallery in Cadnant Road, Menai Bridge was established some ten years ago with the purpose of ensuring a high standard of the visual arts. The works of permanent artists are on view, and several one-man exhibitions are staged through the year. The Tegfryn Art Gallery was opened in part of the home of Mr and Mrs H. J. Brown. It was conceived as a result of a series of exhibitions, and such was the satisfaction to the artists whose work was encouraged, by having a site to exhibit their work, that an extension and a more permanent project seemed essential.

Craft Centre, Cymru, is founded from a group of shops located throughout Wales. Today, the project is established on a sound and solid business foundation. Emphasis is placed on the sale of crafts made in Wales. Traditional Welsh tapestry is a speciality in the merchandise. This league of firms was inspired by the chairman and founder of the shops, David Lewis, who had the insight and the foresight to raise Welsh craftsmanship from its static, if flourishing current state to a first class and international status.

Craft Centre, Cymru, went forward to update products made in Wales, and to enter different kinds of markets.

The ethnic appeal of the products to customers at home and from abroad has been fostered. This has been successful as the demand has grown for good quality, together with a desire to trace a garment back to its source. The important element of individuality is being developed along with the glamour of folk-lore and traditional skills.

2

Textiles

THE WEAVER

PARRY THOMAS, Y GWEHYDD

WOOLCRAFT

Welsh woolcraft, perhaps more than any other, has led the way in the successful revival of modern Welsh crafts. The worth of Welsh wool has been acknowledged nationally through the centuries. Improvements in the breeding of sheep, in spinning and weaving, and in commercial organisation in this century have been such that the wool textile industry is now with the foremost in Wales, and has created a strong international demand. Along with the established woolmark, there is a special Welsh woolmark label bearing the Red Dragon of Wales.

Wisdom and foresight have been shown in preserving the fabrics traditional to Wales. These include frieze cloths, flannels and tapestries. Flannel is one of the earliest of the Welsh cloths, and had for long a world-wide reputation. It was accepted that the Welsh textiles were coarse and rough and heavy in weight, and very durable. Technical processes have ensured that Welsh textiles are now fine, yet durable, of various weights and finishes.

Traditional designs in checks and bold stripes are still available, but there is now an infinite variety of designs in cloths, and even in flannel.

Fashion designers are finding many possibilities for modern Welsh flannel. Tailors are attracted to it, using it for leisure shirts and lightweight jackets.

The lighter Welsh cloths, including a much-sought-after feather weight, have been introduced successfully into women's *haute couture*. Suits, capes, coats, dresses, blouses, slacks and separates are made in soft woollen cloths, and made in dark and pastel colours.

The appeal of Welsh cloth as a furnishing fabric has brought steady revenue to the Welsh mills. Interior designers are aware of its vast possibilities in texture and tone. Welsh tapestry is distinctive. The cloth is warm and durable, and the designs and colours are impressive.

Standard tapestry is, in the terms of the craft, a double cloth. A linear yard weighs approximately 26 ounces. Width varies from 56 to 60 inches. Various wools are used in its manufacture, including imported wool, but with a strong proportion of Welsh wool.

The middle decades of this century have witnessed a remarkable use of Welsh cloth for furnishing purposes. Designers have seen the possibilities of tapestry. The cloth is seen in its excellence as a wall hanging, and as curtains. Used as a floor covering, tapestry is warm and colourful. Upholsterers use double cloth tapestries for upholstering various types of furniture, and also for attractive loose covers.

Woolcraft is one of the oldest in our island. It is highly probable that when the Celtic tribes first settled there were weavers in the small communities that were established. The Welsh verb *gwau* – to weave – has its cognates in other Celtic languages. Much that has passed away elsewhere remains in the textile crafts of Wales, and therefore the study of them is a fertile field, not only for the craftsman, but also for the economist, the historian and the antiquarian.

Throughout mediaeval times, the spinning wheel and the loom

were inseparable from the Welsh hearth. Wool was spun and woven to meet local needs. Craftsmen and craftswomen belonged to the same community as the wearer of the finished goods.

Sheep rearing ranks among the oldest pursuits adopted by civilised man. In the early centuries sheep required constant care and protection from the ravages of wolves and bears. Man came to value the wool of the sheep to a remarkable degree. The woollen industry was guarded by protective laws. When Flemish immigrants settled in Wales under Henry II and Edward III, the Welsh woollen industry was given a strong impetus. The Flemish occupation left distinctive marks on the life and occupations of certain localities especially in Pembrokeshire, Gower and Gwent in the South, and also in some central areas of Wales.

Much cloth was woven in Wales in the fourteenth century. Prosperity attended the craft. An unknown writer of the reign of Elizabeth I urged the development of the woollen industry in Wales – 'I thincke and judge that God and nature hathe appoynted th'inhabitants of Those partes to lyve by cloathing onely'. In the reign of James I, an Act was passed for the Free Trade in Welsh Cloths. The preamble of this Act throws light on the industry in Wales. It states :

'Trade of making Welsh cloths, Cottons, Frezes, linings and plains within the Principality and Dominion of Wales is, and hath been of long continuance; in the using and exercising whereof many thousands of the Poorer Sort of the Inhabitants there in the Precedent Ages, have been set on work of Spinning, Carding, Weaving, Frilling, Cottoning and Shering whereby (having free liberty to sell them to whom and where they would) not only relieved and maintained themselves and their families in good sort, but also grew to such Wealth and Means of Living as they were thereby enabled to pay and discharge all Duties, Mizes, Charges, Subsidies and Taxation, which were upon them imposed or rated in their several Counties, Parishes and Places wherein they dwelled for the Relief of the Poor, and for the service of the King and Commonwealth.'

Contemporary Welsh literature has frequent reference to the woollen industry which was, by its organisation, so closely inter-woven with family life. Constant praise was bestowed on '*brethyn glan y defaid mân*' which was fashioned into clothing.

Travellers in Wales in the seventeenth and eighteenth centuries – men such as Defoe, Mathews, Arthur Young, Pococke and Pennant, testify to the universal use of Welsh cloth. What has come to be regarded as the national dress of the women of Wales, is believed to have been introduced into the country at the close of the eighteenth century. Homespun featured largely in this costume, in the generous skirt, in the *pais a betgwn*, and in the accessories. A scarlet whittle was worn across the shoulders, and fastened in front with a blackthorn prickle.

The carding, spinning, weaving or knitting of wool formed the leisure-hour occupations of Welsh families. Children were recruited to the simpler tasks and were apprenticed to the more intricate processes at an early age. The craft served primarily *local* needs. At times there was a surplus; then dealers carried loads of finished goods on pack horses to the main markets on the Welsh border, such as Shrewsbury, and to seasonal fairs in England. Welsh flannel attained a national reputation. With the growth of the British Empire, this reputation became international. Welsh flannel was worn by many a fur hunter in Canada, and many a miner in Australia and California.

Woolcraft workers in Wales had to face major issues with the coming of the Machine Age. Wool mules and power looms were introduced and craftsmen had to change their outlook, and adapt themselves to changing conditions. The tardiness with which the country adopted the new machines gave a lead in the industry to Yorkshire workers. Militating against the development of the woollen industry in Wales was the opening of mines and industrial valleys, whither people flocked, deserting the rural and less accessible areas. The independent temperament of the Celt may have gravitated against his ready acceptance of the factory system.

It was almost inevitable that a craft so closely associated with the hearth should weave itself into the warp and weft of peasant life. Woolcraft had an ethnic influence. Place names throughout the countryside still testify to the universality of the craft. *Pandy* preserves the name of the fulling mill. *Cwm Twcwr* commemorates the tucker; *clwyf yr edau wlan* – the disease of the woollen thread – was the name given to a type of jaundice. Spinning and weaving were themes of folk song and sermons.

In the first quarter of the twentieth century the woollen industry experienced many vicissitudes, and suffered severely from national

economic depression. Clinging closely to old methods, Welsh craftsmen had been slow to take advantage of the new devices. Moreover,
Wales was poor financially; it lacked capitalists ready to enter into
new enterprises. When machinery was eventually bought, it was
often old-fashioned. As a result, much of the material woven was
sent to England if a fine finish was required, or sent to Scotland if
it was to be dyed.

CARDING AND SPINNING

The whirr of the wool wheel was a familiar sound in Welsh farmhouses and cottages until the Machine Age. Before the wool could
be used for the spinning wheel, the sheep were washed in the mountain streams and then they were sheared. The fleeces were sorted
out according to the length and texture of the wool. In its matted
form the wool was of no use. Therefore, it had to be carded so that
all the fibres were set in the same direction, and 'slives' were formed.
Carding was a tedious process, and so women liked to gather in
'carding bees'.

The wool to be carded was greased very thoroughly. Fat, usually
that of pork, was added to the wool, in the proportion of one-third
to the weight of the wool. The carded wool was made into spindles.
Originally carders were made from teazles known as *llysiau'r
cribau*; they were grown specially for the purpose. Carding combs,
fashioned locally, were also used. They were made from two pieces
of wood – thin but strong. Very fine wire teeth were fitted on one
side of the wood, and a handle was fixed to the side. The wool was
placed between the carding combs. The worker rested the comb
on her knee, and usually held it with her left hand. A hank of wool
was placed on the comb, then the worker drew another carding
comb over the wool, and allowed it to catch in the fine teeth. The
upper comb was warmed from time to time, and then drawn across
the lower carding comb, until the fibres of the wool lay parallel. By
a dextrous turn of the hand and wrist, the wool was gathered into
rolls. When carded to satisfaction, the wool was placed in a box, or
rolled up in a blanket, which was pinned with a blackthorn to await
spinning.

Spinning was the next process and this too was mainly in the
hands of women. The name spinster has become associated with a
woman. Although a spinning wheel was a familiar sight in a Welsh
home, not everyone could spin. It required a diligent apprenticeship

to spin well. The work was highly skilled, demanding sureness and swiftness of eye and hand to ensure uniformity of texture. A spinner aimed at doing a stint of spinning daily.

Spinning wheels are of different types, but the two types in general use in Wales were (a) the kind which had a horizontal spindle and was turned by a wheel fitted with a strap, and (b) the type worked by a treadle. *Y droell fawr* or *y droell fach* was always at hand in the living room for the looms were continuously voracious for spun wool. As with carding, women often got together to spin, and then pitted themselves against each other in speed and skill, in order to get the work done. It was usual for a woman to stand at her spinning wheel, and she aimed at a daily stint of six skeins of yarn. She stepped backward and forward as she worked. A big house might have a spinning gallery; more usually, a Welsh woman worked in her kitchen. It is estimated that many a spinner's steps amounted to as much as 20 miles in a day. Most of the spinning was done for household needs. Spinners were sometimes employed to do the work, but payment was poor.

The spinner placed an end of the carded wool on to the spindle and set the large wheel in motion. The wheel was light. A strap made from woollen yarn passed over the wheel and also over the whorl affixed to it. The spinner gave the big wheel a quick turn, and drew out the wool as it was twisted. By pulling out the wool she regulated the strength and thickness of the twist. The whole process was dependent on the inter-rotary action of the wheel and the whorl. As the wheel whorled, the spinner stepped back. When the twist was of a satisfactory texture, she transferred it to the spindle.

Once the spindle was full, the yarn was removed and run on to a clock reel. This reel was fitted with a device which made a clear clicking sound when forty threads or a knot had been wound on it. Seven knots made a skein. A 'pound' of wool wavered in weight, but rule-of-thumb measures were usually to the buyer's good. The term *pwysgwr*, applied in certain areas to a pound of wool, may have derived from the words *pwys gywir* (full pound), which suggests that the interpretation of a pound may at times have been less or more than the standard weight.

When the wool had been spun, it had next to be spun into two- or three-ply yarn. The process resembles that of spinning. Two strands or three were hooked on to the spindle and coils of thread were placed in a basket on the floor. Rovings were pieces of yarn used from the first spinning. They were used for weaving and for certain types of coarse knitting. When long staple wool was used for this, it was spun with the natural oil of the wool in it, and its waterproof nature was considered an asset for knitted garments that were subject to use in wet weather. Sometimes rovings were turned into firm and durable yarn by being spun a second time on *y droell fach*, or small spinning wheel.

When wound around bobbins the wool could not be dyed. It was necessary to wind it into hanks. Special wool-winders were made for the purpose. Another method was to fix pegs into alternative spokes of the spinning wheel and wind the yarn into a hank around them.

WEAVING

The actual process of weaving is simple and is of great antiquity. Preparing the yarn to its pattern was the most intricate part of the work.

In early days a simple loom was used. Cloth of narrow width was woven. The weaver was dependent on one pair of hands. He threw his shuttle at a range of about 27 inches. Ancient costumes, as illustrated in early manuscripts, show materials of narrow width. When man's ingenuity produced a wider loom, two weavers worked. The shuttle was adapted to throw a wider 'fly' in order to produce cloth of double width. This, in its turn, had its effect on contemporary costume.

Cloth guilds regulated the standard, the width and texture of cloth woven in the towns. Their enforcements doubtless had their effect on the work of the rural weavers. Standard measures were established, and the fixing of the length of a yard did away with the dubious computation of an archer's arm length, which had formerly served to interpret the yard measure.

Weaving looms were an essential part of household equipment. They were often heavy and cumbersome. They stood in a low shed or lean-to outhouse known as *ty'r gŵydd*. The frame was built of timber. It had a big warp beam on which the finished fabric was rolled. The warp was threaded through the harnesses, which were linked with foot treadles. When the weaver trod on a treadle, alternate threads of the warp were lowered. A shed was thus made, and the shuttle bearing the filling was passed through. When the treadle was pressed again, the alternate threads of the warp were lowered and the shuttle was passed back. As weaving frames were developed, they were classified according to their harness. Looms were classified as two-three, four-eight harness looms. A six-harness and an eight-harness loom could produce cloth bearing intricate patterns.

Weaving demanded skill and perseverance, both in the threading of the loom and in the actual weaving of the cloth. These processes took considerable time. Once the loom was threaded, work could go on apace. The same pattern was sometimes woven for months, since there was difficulty in tying on new warp threads. Further, the same pattern was sometimes woven into a fabric of different texture by this method.

Blankets and carthenni (decorative blankets) were given a fringe. Originally, this was because of a desire to use up the remainder of the warp which was fixed to a beam of the loom. Experimenting with the knotting of threads resulted in pleasing fringes.

Much of the weaving was done by women, but in certain localities men were usually weavers. Some were itinerant weavers; they travelled from croft to croft preparing the looms, sometimes giving instructions regarding new crafts and patterns. The actual weaving, after setting up the warp, consisted of filling in the weft by means of a batten or heddle. This final process consisted of taking up the fabric and releasing the warp.

Woollen cloth of good standard was sent to the fuller. The fulling mill was called a *pandy*. Water power was used in such fulling mills, long before it was used for other processes in wool craft. The purpose of sending the cloth to the fuller was to ensure a fine finish. The fuller used fuller's earth, pressing out the natural oil which remained in the wool, and shrinking the material. The fuller dampened the cloth, and then sprayed it with liquid soap. It was then immersed in water and hammered between fulling stocks for two or three more days. By general calculation, cloth shrank by one fourth of its original length. During the process it was removed five or six times and opened and re-opened, and folded and re-folded. When it was sufficiently shrunk it was stretched on a frame set up in the open. It was attached to these tenterposts by tenterhooks fastened to the selvedge of the cloth, and left to dry for three or four days.

The cloth was next pressed between two iron sheets. Heavy

weights were placed on the upper sheet, and the whole was placed near a fire of peat, or logs, or cow dung, so that the material could dry. If a nap was required on the material, this was achieved with the help of teazles (*llysiau'r cribau*). The teazles were placed on a frame and the surface of the cloth, now stretched, was teazed or scratched with the teazles. An assistant workman pushed forward the cloths from the back, so that they could receive the full impact of the teazle heads.

DYEING

Dyes used in olden days were obtained from vegetable sources. Their softness of tone and wide range of colours make some of the old woollen materials of Wales resemble those masterpieces of fine colour produced by the tapestry workers of France and Flanders, the damask weavers of Venice, the embroiderers of Japan, and the woollen spinners of Roubaix and Lille. The discovery of synthetic dyes made the dyer's work less arduous; but the true craftsman knows that from vegetable matter he can produce an infinitude of tints which no money can buy. Moreover, in preserving the traditions of old art, and in recognising the necessity of forming an insoluble lac in the fibre of the material by the combination of a suitable metallic salt with the natural dye base, he knows he may evolve a number of fresh dyes and original tints. Much of the fastness of the peasant dyes was due to precision, a meticulous art, and habit, of taking pains in the process of dyeing.

Brown dyes were obtained from Persian berries and Brazil wood. Their sober tones were largely used in dying woollen goods. Cloths were dyed solid, but tweeds were woven from yarns in which the colours had been blended during the carding process, thus forming a mixture in the finished cloth. Buffs and tans were often used in conjunction with brown. These were obtained by using weak baths of brown dyes, or old baths that had been used. Black lichen, *parmelia sexitilis*, yielded buffs and browns. This lichen, sometimes known as crotal, is common enough on the Welsh moors and bogs. It spreads like a black sponge on the rocks and boulders, and can be collected easily. Another lichen, the *ramalina fraxina*, is found in abundance on the cliffs of the West coast, and on the bark of oak trees. When wool or cloth was subjected to mordanting first, modified tones were procured from the lichens. Green, yellow and red tones were thus made possible.

Heather yielded golden yellow dyes. These were made easily. The leaves, flowers and terminal twigs of heather and ling were cut up and boiled, with correct proportions of alum, tartar and water. Old gold yellow was made by altering the proportions and very fine orange tints were made by combining the yellow dye with madder. Sulphate of iron added to the heather bath produced an olive green colour. Fustic, tumeric, ebony and wild mignonette and yellow broom also yielded yellow dyes. Red was obtained with the aid of a little grub called cochineal, which supplied dyes for the scarlet coats of the army. Today this dye is more familiar in the making of confectionery.

Direct dyeing in cochineal produced crimson and purples; cloth which had been mordanted, however, produced different tones. Scarlet was obtained by adding oxymuriate of tin to the cochineal extract. Crimson resulted from the combination of cochineal with alum; orange-red tints were produced by a mixture of cochineal and cream of tartar, and purple was achieved by mixing alkaline salts with the extract.

Cudbear allied to other lichens or sulphates produced a wide range of maroon dyes ranging from light bright tints to dark sombre colours.

Logwood chips, producing a rich red colour, and pearlash – i.e. impure carbonate of soda – used in varying quantities along with sulphate of copper, produced beautiful tones of grey.

Indigo and woad yielded blue dyes. Fermentation of the leaves of these plants used severally produced an insoluble dark blue powder. The dyer showed his skill in rendering the powder into soluble dye.

Greens were made by combining yellows and blues, and were also produced directly from the leaves and stems of the coltsfoot (*tussilago farfara*) which grows in abundance in waste places in Wales.

Seaweed, soot, shells, the fruit and leaves of the blackberry and black currant, the ubiquitous mountain ash fruit, onion skins, the bark of the elder tree were used for making dyes, and some of these were used as mordants. The dye pot was boiled over a peat fire in many areas. A wooden board pierced with holes served as a cover. The mixture was stirred as it boiled. The dampened wool or cloth was immersed in the dye, and salt was added to set the colour. The wool was rinsed in a mountain rill and then hung out to dry.

The vegetable dyes produced colours of a natural softness, reminiscent of the countryside wherein they were created.

KNITTING

Excellent knitting wools are prepared in the Welsh mills. They are well known for their virtues of resistance to shrinkage and felling in the face of severe treatment.

There are fine one-ply yarns coming off the same sheep; they match up with the bulkier wools now knitted into fashionable heavy-knit garments. There is a wide range of colouring – mint green, browns and browns blended with black; then there is a lovely range of colourings of rose, violet, periwinkle, and blue-green blends.

Many mills supply tweeds and worsteds which are perfectly matched to knitting wools.

Before the Machine Age the click of the knitting needles was a usual accompaniment to the life of a Welshwoman from early childhood to old age. As a child she learnt to knit long before she learnt to read. Her first irregular stitches were an essay at the creation of knitted garments. Later, she progressed to the knitting of the stockings. Hand-knitted stockings were an essential part of Welsh dress up to the close of the eighteenth century. Women knitted stockings for the family. Grey, black or dark blue were used for men. Children wore red stockings. Women chose yarns of colour appropriate to their ensemble. Sombre shades were favoured as the result of the chastening influence of the religious revivals of the eighteenth century.

Knitting was a branch of woolcraft and could be regarded as forming part of one of the staple Welsh industries. In hard times every member of the family, men as well as women, knitted. Stocking money was in many localities devoted to the payment of rent. Knitting was a craft which could be carried on in most places excepting church. Knitted garments were characterised by their durability, variety and beauty.

Fleecy wools were knitted into the shawls which were so important a feature of the traditional Welsh costume.

Traditional patterns characterised most knitted fabrics, including counterpanes and rugs. Among the designs were the fan pattern, in its many varieties, a peacock's tail, the leaf, the square, and the hexagonal block. Some of these were incorporated in knitted lace.

This was worked with large needles, and used to adorn counter-panes, table coverings, etc.

The accessories of the craft were few, and knitting bees had social as well as functional value.

Just as the home knitter of today values the economic worth of a garment on which she has expended her time and labour, so, too, did the Welshwoman of the past set an economic and financial assessment on her craft.

The traditional national costume of Wales makes extensive use of *brethyn cartre'* – homespun cloth. Hand-knitted stockings are accessories.

It was usual to see the menfolk take up knitting when manual work for the day was over. They were pressed into service when a special fair or market day was approaching. The men would help the women of the household to complete a dozen or more pairs of stockings for the stocking merchant, the famed *saneuwr*. The payment for these hand-knitted stockings was very poor. At the close of the nineteenth century, the price averaged from ten pence to a shilling a pair. Good knitting was essential, or else the *saneuwr* would refuse to accept the stockings. Fine workmanship was not possible at such cheap rates. Consequently, one-ply yarn, knitted on coarse needles in loose stitches was used for *sanau gwerthi* – the stockings made for selling. Stockings of this type could not be subjected to hard wear. They were suitable for town-dwellers not engaged in manual work.

For home wear, the womenfolk knitted stockings of a more durable quality. They knew that only stockings knitted on fine needles, using three-ply yarn of good quality, were suitable for rural work, where men wore heavy boots or clogs.

Hugh Evans writing in *The Gorse Glen* relates a poignant tale which serves to illustrate the value of knitting to a household in the hard years of the nineteenth century:

'This is the story Richard Jones told . . .

'When I was a little boy, I well remember how my mother kept my father and all the family from starvation during one year. Owing to a late harvest and bad weather, when it was time to carry the corn, practically all of it had rotted in the fields that year. What remained was bad or useless, except to feed the pigs with. Grain was very dear, and we had no money to buy any. There were hundreds of families in Wales in the same case, winter coming on and famine staring us in the face. My father nearly went mad thinking of the black winter that faced us.

'One night my mother broke the heavy silence, and said to my father "I'll make a bargain with thee; I'll see to the food for us both and the children all winter, if thou, in addition to looking after the cattle and the pigs, wilt do the churning, wash up, make the beds and clean the house. I'll make the butter myself."

' "How wilt thou manage?", asked my father, with the tears running down his cheeks.

' "I will knit", said she. "We have wool. If thou wilt card it, I will spin."

'The bargain was struck; my father did the housework in addition to the work of the farm, and my mother knitted. She rose early and worked late, and out of the twenty-four hours she only slept five or six. She had set herself the task of knitting three stockings a day.

'Once in each fortnight my mother would go on horseback to Ruthin, over Mynydd Hiraethog, a distance of some fifteen miles, with her bundle of stockings to sell to the stocking man. With the money she got for her stockings, she would purchase a peck of barley, bringing it home with her to be ground to make food for us. And so it was that she kept us alive until the next harvest.

'It should be remembered that people at that time did not wear short socks, but stockings that came over the knee, measuring nearly three feet from top to toe.'

Earlier Arthur Aiken, writing an account of his *Tour Through North Wales* (1797), referred to knitting as being

'the general leisure work of both sexes, and it cannot fail of giving strangers a high idea of the industry of the people to see the men and women going to market with burdens on their heads, while their hands are employed in working the fleeces of their own sheep, into articles of dress.'

Knitted hose was sold in fairs.

Writing in *The History of the Honourable Society of Cymmrodorion 1751–1951*, Helen Ramage and R. T. Jenkins state:

'A poorer relation of the drover was the "*hosier*", the seller of stockings. Of the tripod on which the economy of the older Welsh countryside was somewhat precariously supported in pre-industrial ages, agriculture proper was one leg, livestock the second, and wool the third. Welsh "webs" and "flannels" were marketed by English middle-men. But the knitted wares were a different matter; here the whole process from sheep to retail was domestic. Welsh hosiers (women even more than men) travelled enormous distances on foot (and bare-footed) with their stock slung over their shoulders. They were known in London Town, where some of them indeed settled down, rose from peddling, and became solid tradesmen.'

The crafts are inextricably linked with culture and social life, particularly in a rural community.

In *The Gorse Glen* – *Cwm Eithin*, Hugh Evans recorded an account of a knitting night as kept in North Wales in the mid-nineteenth century. The social value of the custom, in addition to its economic worth, is apparent. He wrote:

'I do not know whether the custom was general throughout Wales, but it was certainly known in Llanuwchllyn, where, for some reason I cannot explain, it was called a *ffram*. It is said that the famous old preacher, Dafydd Cadwaladr, learnt to read from the pitch letters on the sheep of his old home, Erw Dinmael, and that by the time he had become a farm lad in Nant y Cyrtiau, he could repeat Ellis Wynne's *Bardd Cwsc*, and the Welsh translation of Bunyan's *Pilgrim's Progress*, from memory. In Cwm Tir Mynach in those days, he was invited to one knitting night after another to recite portions of those books. This speaks pretty well for the intellectual standards of the district at that time. . . . The old custom was rapidly falling into disuse in my time, although I can remember an occasional *noswaith weu* being held. The lecture, the concert, and the competitive meeting were just beginning to find a footing in the locality, and the older forms of entertainment were rather frowned upon. Still, I have a clear recollection of a knitting night held in my own home when I was a small boy, my grandmother presiding. . . . She invited all the young women and the young men to a *noswaith weu*. I believe it was the last of its kind in *Cwm Eithin*, and it may well have been the last in Wales. The nearest approach to it in our day is the fashionable *At Home*. . . .

'When it was settled to have a *noswaith weu*, the first step to decide was whom to invite, the number of course depending upon the size of the house, and the host's resources. On *the* day, the housewife would be kept busy all afternoon making light cakes, baking another cake on the grid, and packing the children off to the village to buy a white loaf and a pound of loaf sugar. The guests were usually young people, both male and female. The girls arrived first, and it was considered the proper thing for the young men to linger a little before putting in an appearance. When all had come, the womenfolk would begin to knit, and one or two lads, inveterate jokers, would also produce needles and yarn and begin to knit garters. To tell the truth, there was not very much solid work done at a *noswaith weu*, as so much time was spent in laughing at the stories and picking up the stitches, after the lads had plucked them out.

'A good story-teller was always in demand for these occasions, and some of them had a great store of tales of the *Tylwyth Teg* and other fairies. These had their effect; they amused the company, and they made the girls far too nervous to be able to walk home without a male escort. The *noswaith weu* was a great clearance house for local gossip, and for rumours of courtship. Sometimes the invitations would be so arranged, that a couple who were suspected to be courting would be invited, and the reactions when they met and talked to each other would be watched by keen and interested eyes.'

The economic worth of the craft, however, remained paramount. Hugh Evans, a keen observer, recorded:

'The knitting of stockings was an important part of women's work, and often enough, the men could knit also. The stocking merchant, *saneuwr*, attended all the fairs and markets, buying the stockings in the local fairs and re-selling them in the large centres. . . . I can remember a time when my grandmother sold men's stockings for eleven pence and for a shilling a pair. Tears come into my eyes every time I read Tom Hood's *The Song of the Shirt*, and I thank God, that our mothers, in all their poverty did not have to live in the large English towns. They had, at least, the blue sky over their heads, the green grass for a carpet under their feet, and the clean air of the countryside to breathe, and, poor as they were, they had something better than a bed of straw to lie on. Their beds of chaff were clean and soft. I am thankful, too, that their work was knitting and not sewing; they had not to sit stooping over their work in dark rooms; they could knit while in the fields with the scent of the wild flowers in their nostrils.

'My grandmother and my mother could knit quite rapidly, while reading the Bible on the little round table by their side, and sometimes as they read and knitted, they sang of the promise of God.' (*The Gorse Glen.*)

WOOL RUG-MAKING

The creation of rugs at home is a domestic craft which has in it the element of folk art. From the time when the Welshman built his *tyddun un-nos*, the small freehold cottage built overnight, he showed a strong desire to own his home, however humble. With this went a pride to adorn the house. Man and wife were imbued with a desire for things beautiful within the home. There was a desire for refinement and comfort.

The floors of raftered kitchens were covered with hand-made rugs. Some of these were braided, the plaiting being inspired by straw work. Rugs thus made were durable and washable. They were cheap; old garments served as material. Dark colours were enlivened by richer tones, and the housewife showed her ingenuity by dyeing. Mosses and berries yielded dyes of subtle tones and lasting quality. A finished rug often displayed a galaxy of colours and, like the patchwork quilt, it was a repository of sentiment.

Hooked rugs were made. Canvas or coarse burlap formed the ground; patterns were outlined roughly on the foundation. These patterns were crude, but had astonishing vitality.

The cottager's love for her garden and its beds and borders of flowers was apparent in the rugs that she hooked. Pinks and Sweet Williams and roses were often massed together, and floral designs were sometimes copied from elaborate embroidery work.

Geometrical designs were worked. These had close affinity with the pitched floors and pavements of many Welsh homes.

Sailors sometimes helped in rug making. Their designs were reminiscent of the sea. Fish swam confidently between borders of seaweed and shell. Ships voyaged safely beneath the lettering of appropriate texts.

Shawl patterns were copied on to rugs. Occasionally, a familiar landscape or homestead was designed on the canvas, and the finished product was valued for its sentiment, if not for its scale and accuracy.

QUILTING

Quilting is practised by many women in Wales, mainly for personal use. They have given fresh life to traditional craft by adapting it to modern needs. The craftswomen no longer confine themselves to the making of quilted bed covers. Their work now includes cot quilts, cushion covers, dressing gowns, jackets and slippers. A distinct advance came with the creation of articles to meet specific demands for modern interior decoration. Such work has at times been done communally.

Quilting designs have been passed down from one generation to another. It is a form of needlecraft which has received special emphasis in Wales. The high standard of work and the beauty of patterns created in the past have inspired workers of the present age.

The quilt developed with the evolution of the bedstead. While the box bed prevailed, there was little need or opportunity for using or displaying fine quilts. The box bed was warm. Coverings were few and were not displayed. The truckle bed, when not in use, was usually pushed under a large bed. It was usually relegated to a child or servant, and was not given special attention.

With the advent of the tester or tent bed in the seventeenth century, quilts assumed a prominent place. Among the richer classes – the nobility, the merchants and the landed gentry, quilts became articles of acknowledged worth, ranging with articles of furniture, as is testified by old wills and inventories. In the old coaching days, when accommodation was limited, beds were of a tremendous size. They could occasionally sleep ten or twelve – witness the Bed of Ware. Coverings were made to an appropriate size.

In earlier centuries the word quilting referred to a form of needlecraft, rather than to the bed-covering. From the sixteenth to the early nineteenth centuries quilting appeared on the clothing of both men and of women. Men had worn quilted jerkins under their coats of mail in the Middle Ages. In post-feudal days they wore doublets and knee breeches which were quilted. Fashionable ladies wore quilted coats and skirts. Queen Elizabeth wore them. Her mother, Anne Boleyn, received a gift of several bed quilts, from Henry VIII. Were these, we wonder, inspired by Welsh craftsmanship? The real answer we shall never know, for by their nature quilts are perishable.

The quilted petticoat remained in favour down to the Regency period. The popularity of quilted garments was accounted for by their durability and warmth. Many a Welsh chatelaine, in a highland manor house, must have treasured the possession of an heirloom quilted petticoat. Even in the late nineteenth century, the quilted petticoat was fashionable in Wales. New fashions seeped westward but slowly. A desire strong and traditional among women folk was to be buried in a petticoat of black satin, elaborately quilted. In this way countless fine specimens, treasured, unworn in a house for a generation or more, were committed to the earth in full solemnity of the burial service. The custom links the Welsh peasant with that of Scandinavia, where, in youth, a young woman designed and embroidered elaborate clothes for her burial.

Where there was poverty, self-respect was maintained by the use of what might also be termed a communal burial petticoat. These were in black; sometimes in brown; they were used for laying-out the dead. Such petticoats were preserved for a long period of time.

The craft owes its strength however, to the quilt as a bed covering.

Most young women learnt the art of quilting. Every self-respecting bride prided herself on her set of six or more quilts, made partly, at least, with her own hands. She had them in readiness for entry into her new home. Every self-respecting widow could rely on her own skill as a quilt wife, if she had to meet the economic exigencies of a cruel world.

The craft was regarded as a pleasant one; the fundamentals were easily mastered. Three layers of material were stitched together. The top layer was often chosen for its fine texture and attractive pattern. There were quilts of taffeta and also of fine linen, though cotton or sateen were more usual. Sometimes a fine lining was placed to support the surface cloth if it was of an open texture. The lin-

ing was of cheap cotton material. The padding was of cotton wool;
sometimes a worn blanket was used. For a cot quilt, wool would be
gathered from the hedgerows. A material which was less elaborate
was usually placed on the bottom surface. To manipulate the work
with ease, the materials were stretched on a rectangular wooden
frame, set horizontally. The ends of the quilts were wrapped around
the frame which was covered with flannel. It was unrolled as
needed.

The quilting frame was a familiar sight in the window nook of
the kitchen in farmhouse or cottage. Its social significance in traditional life would make an interesting study. In its own way, the
quilting frame compared with the blacksmith's smithy as an unofficial parliament where public opinion was forged, questioned and
sometimes denounced. The quilt wife's craft symbolised much that
was vital and invigorating in the life of the countryside.

A bride-to-be would announce a quilting 'bee' or meeting in her
home. She took care to choose a day that would best fit in with
the demands of a rural community. When hay-making was over,
or harvest was in, or when a Saint's day gladdened the dreary winter
calendar, then the women of the district were well pleased to answer the call to the quilting bee.

The women would assemble in the bride's house. If a quilt was
not already begun, they would set to work to put in place the long
rectangular frames. They would place a layer of flannel on the long
beams, place the layers of cloth in position, and then raise the
frame for easy manipulation, resting it on four chairs. The hostess
would have all the implements ready at hand. These were few in
number, comprising thread, needles, scissors, and perhaps templates.

The design itself had probably been chosen well beforehand, so
now came an interval of approbation or discussion. When plans
were agreed upon some of the women set to work. Quilting stitches
are few in number. Care has to be taken that the stitches go through
all layers. Running stitch, back stitch, chain stitch, cat-a-cornered,
and herring stitch were among the most usual. The quilt wife sought
not so much to display the stitch itself, as to use it to throw into
relief the padded design.

Work was started at the centre of the quilt, and progressed outwards. When a section of the quilt had been finished it was opened
out; she who had completed her design first would be the first to

be married. When the quilt was taken from its frame, it was shaken and duly admired. The men folk would arrive to partake of a special supper, and gay conviviality graced the scene.

If quilting stitches were few in number, traditional designs were very numerous. Special attention was given, not only to designs as units, but also to their assembling to ensure an effective arrangement. Remarkable precision of eye was evident. Many quilt wives scorned the template, scorned even the slight marking of the material with the needle's point. Less skilled women used wooden templates, heavily chalked on their rims, and pressed on the quilt as was needed. An ever-ready template was a saucer. Its edge was greased. This was used to create intricate chains, scallops or curves.

Geometric patterns were also used. Straight lines were assembled in intricate patterns. Many of these are still prevalent as diagonal designs – single, double, triple and quadruple. They form diamonds, stars, and broken plaid patterns. Curved lines developed naturally. They had picturesque names such as ocean wave, true lovers' knots, tulip and feather designs. Other quilt designs which became traditional were Star of Bethlehem, Lone Star, Seven Stars, Noah's Dove, Rose of Sharon, Rising Sun, and Hour Glass.

PATCHWORK QUILTS

When a housewife wanted to make up a bedcover cheaply and quickly, she turned to patchwork. Pieces of cotton material were sewn together, sometimes with very little consideration for colour or design.

Patchwork, however, could serve as a fitting vehicle for the craftswoman's skill. The patchwork quilt could be the most valuable bed-covering in the housewife's chest. Her collection of patches often had pieces of sentimental worth. Into her quilt she sewed sections of her confirmation dress, her wedding gown, her child's christening gown, and material exchanged with friends. Such treasured pieces were not just sewn together haphazardly : they were cut artistically and arranged in designs. Sometimes they were just formed together; more frequently, they were mounted on to a base of unbleached calico or similar material. The covering would serve as the top layer of a quilt. Sometimes it was left as it was placed on the padding; sometimes it was quilted.

Designs were traditional in a district. There was a great galaxy from which to choose. Basket patterns were prime favourites for they were comparatively easy. Fan designs were also popular, and Irish chain. Log cabin designs demanded careful work, but were esteemed as well worth the extra effort.

Patchwork designs were sometimes appliquéd on to the foundation material, or, more usually, on to plain squares of white calico or coloured print. Flower and leaf designs were also popular. The oak leaf, the lily, and the rose, were also popular in Wales.

PATCHWORK TODAY

In rural Mid-Wales, at Noyadd Rhulen, near Builth Wells, patchwork is now made in various shapes, particularly in an intriguing shell-shape, and cut from charming and colourful cottons. Much is being made into house furnishings; these include curtains, wall hangings, cushion covers, bedspreads and cot covers.

The interest in patchwork is perennial. As genuinely antique patchwork becomes exceedingly rare, modern initiative finds expression in creating new ones and meeting a demand. Today, whether made individually or as group work, it is made in designs of such charm and character that it will survive in its own right, and become in itself, a heirloom of the future.

At Noyadd Rhulen, patchwork has in it the elements of a cottage industry. Sound organisation is behind the enterprise. The shell-shape patchwork is sewn by women working in their own homes. Some work is done by hand in the traditional fashion; some is machine-sewn.

The directors set a high standard of work. It is they who are responsible for the striking designs; it is they who ensure that each product created has charm and individuality. Cotton fabrics are used. As many as twenty different patterns of fabric are used in a single size bed cover.

There is artistry in the creation of the shell-shapes, which are approximately 12 inches in diameter. The patchwork is lined with heavy unbleached calico; corded edges give a firm finish.

Covers are made in country style, and are individually designed. Materials are fresh and pretty, the whole being surrounded by a 12-inch border of gingham. The bed covers are also made as padded quilts. Striking colours are chosen for duvet covers.

The shell-shaped patchwork is far more difficult to sew than the more traditional hexagonal patchwork. The making of the shell-shapes is a real labour of love.

Patchwork is also made into curtains with dramatic designs, into cushions of various sizes and purpose, and for cot covers. Smaller articles included tea-cosies and egg-cosies. Of very special appeal are men's ties, and beautiful skirts for evening wear.

3

Stone

SAER MAEN • THOMAS GORDON DAVIES • MASON

The hard granite and slate found in North and in Mid-Wales, and the renowned grey-blue stone from the Presceli Hills of Dyfed, have been valued by craftworkers through the centuries. Their rugged and hard-wearing qualities have been proved. In past centuries, stonemasons built cathedrals and monasteries and churches. Much ecclesiastical work, and in especial, repair work is done today. Workers in stone have adapted their craft to modern needs, creating plaques and ornaments for civic and garden use. One such craftsman is Maurice Riley, of Clegyr Isaf, St David's, a stone mason, banker and fixer. Banker mason is a mediaeval term for bench worker and highly skilled carver. The word banker is self-explanatory in the craft, covering all fields of carved work.

Nowadays Maurice Riley uses modern diamond tools and chisels. These are expendable and have tungsten tips. In the past, the blacksmith who could make a suit of armour, the steel hammered to perfection, made chisels which were hammered to a mason's individual requirements.

He is a man who loves his craft, and who is fighting actively for its survival and true evaluation. His philosophy of life, as well as his handiwork cannot but arouse admiration.

Maurice Riley remains true to his training in craftemanship. Whatever the economics of the situation, he is determined to keep the craft alive. He has agitated constantly in places of authority against the reduction in time served by apprentices. He maintains steadfastly that hard work is the keystone to a sound society. To give reward without effort is a retrograde step in civilisation.

Like many discriminating stone masons, Maurice Riley has a predeliction for local stone. At the present time, the country is flooded with stone from South Africa, the Balkan countries, and Sweden. It is machine cut, and carries a mirror-like polish. It is prepared so that it will not age and become weather beaten, never even grow moss.

Despite his strong advocacy of local stone, Maurice Riley finds that the response is disappointing. Nevertheless, as a true craftsman, his own reward lies in the satisfaction of doing a good job. He has the artist's unmistakable *savoir faire*, a knowledge of what is fitting, of what is harmonious in a building, and an abhorrence of all that is cheap and tawdry.

The Cathedral at St David's is built from local sandstone, known as Caerbwdy Stone. It was brought from the tidal quarry from which it was hewn. It is known to geologists as Cambrian Stone and is found in varying shades of grey to purple. The Cathedral was built over hundreds of years. One of the oldest memorial stones is to a Bristol mason. Stone from Caerbwdy was exported. A great deal went into the building of Strata Florida Abbey, Ceredigion. The last local banker masons were employed by Sir Gilbert Scott in the 1870 and in the 1920 restorations. The success of the brick industry militated against stone dressing, but an upsurge in the appreciation of stonework may well be lying in the near future.

Stone is more than antique. Its years may be counted in millions. The stonework in the cemeteries of the land spell out the history of a village or town. There is a growing appreciation of the value and charm of antique hand-carved work. With it grows a true appraisal of the stone mason's craft. Stonework is hard and tedious work. There is no room for mistakes. The reward is in the finished job.

DRY-STONE WALLING

Dividing the Welsh moorland into intricate patterns are dry-stone hedges, which stand firm against the onslaught of wind and rain. Many have survived for decades and others are good for long service, requiring only the minimum of care. They testify to the ingenuity of the Welsh country craftsman who, without the advantage of technical knowledge, or the assistance of mechanical power, achieved works of art.

The craftsmen made use of local material, turning to the outcrop of rock on the hillside for the stones. In North Wales many of the thin dykes are of blue ragstone taken from the slate quarries; in South-Eastern Wales, in the old red sandstone districts, dykes are thick and heavy. In Central Wales, the dry waller made use of huge rocks of irregular size, obtaining a balance in his wall which appears long afterwards as remarkable. In limestone areas of the West wallers followed the nature of the stone, moulding, in rough fashion, the soft and even grain of the stone into drip stones, which they set as a cornice on the wall to protect it from the almost ceaseless rain borne by the south-west winds.

The dry waller had an instinctive sense, not only of the material at hand to his use, but also of the lie of the land, whereon he planned to build his wall. A rough moorland would not allow a clear line for a dyke; preliminary work had to be done to remove unsightly and provocative boulders. This was sometimes done by blasting, but more usually by boring and wedging, a feat of engineering which the dry waller usually accomplished with the lone help of a boy assistant. Cavities and inclines were made even by filling in with rock debris, which had to have time to set before the stone wall was laid upon it. A greater bugbear to the stone waller was an area of soft marshy ground or peat soil, into which he was obliged to sink a foundation wall of greater depth than the above-surface wall. For such work he was obliged to call in the often grudgingly-given help of farm labourers, who could ill be spared from the toil of the mountain farmstead.

When the land was solid, the dry waller sometimes laid the wall directly on the surface, but more usually he cut a shallow dyke to receive the base of the wall. These turfs cut in the moorland were valued for their fertility, and were conveyed back to the farm when the stones had been unloaded from the cart.

The work of the dry waller was seasonal. Most of the work was done in the spring or in the summer; it was almost impossible to attempt work in the face of snow, bleak winds, and driving rain in the winter months.

Because of the heavy nature of his material, the dry waller kept a shrewd eye on economy in its handling. An old craftsman could give an astonishingly accurate estimate of the amount of stone needed, and an apprentice lad did well to garner such knowledge early in his career. A ton of stone for one square yard was a usual calculation. When the dry waller chose to err on the surplus side, he made sure that his supplies of stones were piled neatly on the higher reaches of the dyke track, so as to facilitate handling.

When blue ragstone is used for walling, the dry-stone waller's purpose is to place the dark blue slate-like stones as flat as possible, following a cord line along the track. The slabs of ragstone are not uniform in size, but he arranges them so, in so far as he can, and they respond fairly readily to the craftsman's strokes. The dry waller's skill is called into play as he cuts water holes on the stones. These are oblique notches on the outer faces of the stones, to ensure that the rain drips outwards.

Walls are usually built double, the dry waller and his lad working on either side of the dyke. Sometimes a rough frame is set up to hold the plumb cord, but an old craftsman tends to set greater worth on the 'feel' of rock, or on accuracy of eye. The two workers build at the same rate, keeping the wall as even as possible. In many areas it is usual to fill the inner section of the wall with loose stones. In the process of building and filling in, it is no small task to lift hundredweights of rough stone and engineer them into position.

Some walls have part fillings of mortar, which have to be both water- and wind-proof. The craftsman places the mortar in the inner regions of the wall only, recognising that it is a waste of labour to place it on the sloping surfaces of the outer stones, where the wind and the rain would soon disperse it.

The wall builder, however, does not place great emphasis on the use of mortar for binding. He knows as surely as did the builder of mediaeval cathedrals that the strength of the wall depends not upon mortar, nor on the thickness of the stones, but in the *direction* in which the stones meet a stress. At intervals stones known as *through* stones are placed in the wall to bind it. Sometimes these are built even with the surface of the wall; sometimes they are longer and jut out on both sides of the boundary wall; or, in the case of a barn or sheepfold, on the outer side of the structure only.

The walls on the Welsh moorland vary considerably. Some are three, some are four, and some are five feet high. The sharp slope of the land may sometimes gravitate against the outward pressure of the weight of the stones; and so the craftsman who takes pride in the strength and endurance of his wall will go back along the long line of his dyke and set up wedge-shaped stones to ensure an end-to-end pressure. Some workmen leave cavities in the wall to receive these buttresses, making ample accommodation to receive them in places showing structural weakness.

When building stone walls on pastoral land, the stone builder will increase their usefulness by setting up small openings within the structure to enable sheep to pass through. A smooth-surfaced stone is fitted in as a lintel, and a rectangular slab or a rounded boulder is placed near the gap to help the sheep passing through. The coping stones themselves, especially those on limestone walls, are often arranged in an alternate pattern of horizontal or vertical stones. Here again the craftsman builds to serve a local need. His coping stones take into consideration the average jump of the mountain sheep, as assuredly as his bridged openings in the wall are built to accommodate their size.

The number of dry wallers in Wales has sadly diminished, but there are prospects of resuscitation. Practical interest is being shown in the craft, and Young Farmers Clubs among other sections of the populace find practical value as well as pleasure in the keen competitions in dry walling.

FLOUR MILLING

At *Felin Wen, White Mill*, a village on the A40 about four miles from Carmarthen, is an old mill which produces stone-ground 100% wholemeal flour.

Heredity plays its part in the ownership and working of the mill.

The family, old-established in Dyfed, has worked the mill since 1815. The fifth generation is now in command.

An earlier member of the family, showing great enterprise, went to the North of England as an apprentice, and qualified as a millwright engineer. In 1846 he took charge of the mill at Felin Wen. He put in new machinery from top to bottom. He replaced the wooden-slatted outside mill wheel with an iron one. This was made to his own design by the Davies Foundry at Cardigan. Six or seven men were employed at the mill in its hey-day. Now three are employed there.

The owner-craftsman is capable of undertaking all the processes at the mill.

The wheat for the wholemeal flour is collected on the Welsh border – Hereford, Gloucester and areas of Wiltshire. Local wheat is too soft for use. Favourable crops are produced in West Wales during a hot summer.

A member of the mill family collects the wheat from the farms in bags. On delivery, it is hauled up to the top of the mill. It is cleaned thoroughly of straw, husk and dirt. It is re-bagged at the bottom of the mill, and hauled back again to the top storey, where it is poured out into the hopper immediately above the large flour stone.

The wheat is then ground up and it passes through a wide chute into a large trough on the ground floor of the mill. Here it is allowed to cool for two or three days before bagging and selling.

The top stone, or runner's stone, which weighs about half a ton, moves clockwise on the bed grindstone. This rubbing action makes the flour. It rubs the grain through races which are cut to a sharpness, so that the wheat flour flowing down into the trough is nice and mealy, and one can see the flakes of bran quite plainly in the flour – and finally in the bread. The action of this stone, which is a special French burr stone, adds to the taste of the final product. Certainly the wholemeal flour from White Mill has its own unique flavour.

The grain must not contain more than 13% moisture. It should be allowed to stand fourteen days before baking.

The old-fashioned packing was best. The flour was filled into hessian bags. The air was able to circulate freely around the bag. The hand-ground flour is full of wheat-germ and makes very good, wholesome food. It is being recommended more and more by the medical world. Nowadays paper bags have to be used to hold the flour.

The millstones have to be dressed every year. It is a great undertaking. The top stone, a burr stone at White Mill, is lifted by means of a wire rope and steel pulley and turned over on blocks. The flour is brushed away carefully, and a rod painted with red-oxide is rubbed across the surface of the stone, and also across the bed-stone, the lower fixed stone in the pair of millstones. Both stones are then chipped by hand with special case-hardened chisels. When there is no trace of red-oxide left on the stones, they are again painted with red-oxide and re-chipped until free of lead paint.

The furrows or races are then cut and painted, so that each furrow is deepened sufficiently to allow the meal to run coolly, and be swept along by the projecting tag to fall through the rectangular opening connecting with a chute which delivers the flour to the trough on the ground floor.

After an interval of a few days the flour is weighed and bagged. It is then sold in neighbouring towns. The mill is a mecca for tourists in the holiday season.

Due to economic and technical difficulties, the picturesque water wheel is not now in use. An engine was installed in 1933. When this was removed it was taken as an exhibit to the Maritime Museum, Swansea. A new air-cooled engine has more recently been installed. This is efficient and satisfactory in the working of the old flour mill.

SLATE

The Tudor Slate Works, Groeslon, Caernarfon was established in 1861. It specialised in producing writing slates, framed in wood, for schools, and also slate pencils. Much of its recent success has lain in adapting itself to meet current demands. The demand for school slates diminished, but slate was required for the electrical industries. Slate switchboards became a speciality. Many of these were for great ships like the *Queen Mary* and *Queen Elizabeth* and the *Mauretania*.

The building industry required slate. Consequently craftsmen were employed in creating cills, copings and facings. Men at Groeslon were commissioned to make a floor for Kensington Palace, and surfaces for de luxe kitchens.

The craftsmen have access to a wide range of machinery, including drills, saws and planes. They can select slate from different quarries at Aberllefenne, Blaenau Ffestiniog, and Penrhyn. Roofing slates continue to be in great demand. The craft items produced are of a high standard. Most have been exhibited at the Design Centre, London. Chess boards and occasional tables are made in slate.

The Llechwedd Slate Quarries, owned by J. W. Greaves and Sons Ltdsince the early nineteenth century, have yielded high quality slate. The deposits are in an area surrounding Blaenau Ffestiniog, in Gwynedd, North Wales. The extraordinary qualities of the slate mined have been recognised from earliest times. The slates produced here became an accepted standard. Such was the demand for the slates that the Company built a private wharf at Portmadoc.

At the same time, the Company takes pride in the fact that ancient techniques for the treating and dressing of slate, which can be traced back to use in Israel more than three thousand years ago, are still in use in the Llechwedd Quarries. These are preserved, for they are unsurpassed for their efficiency. The Company is proud of them as the basis for the remarkable and continuing high quality of Llechwedd products.

Heredity and tradition are much in evidence here. Llechwedd craftsmen are preserving the traditions that their forefathers created. Their skills – and also their culture – are valuable possessions handed down through the generations during the past century and a half.

J. W. Greaves and Company claim that the finest slate in Wales is to be found in the Llechwedd Quarries. It has always been the custom to welcome tourists and mining specialists to the mines. Such has been the response that now there is a Tourist Centre at the mines. The number of visitors who come here from all parts of the world each year is calculated in many thousands. The visitors are taken on a conducted tour underground. They travel through the solid hillside viewing the vast and awesome chambers. After, they watch the craftsmen cutting and dressing the raw slate, and fashioning it into a variety of products. The Craft Shop is the focus of keen attention, for here craftsmen can be seen making decorative articles in slate.

The famous blue-grey Ffestiniog slate comes from the Llechwedd. Maenofferen and Diphwys Slate Mines. Multi-coloured rustic slate is obtained from the Braich Ddu Slate Quarry.

Roofing slate remains the chief product. No finer roofing material has been discovered. It is made in a wide variety of standards, sizes and thicknesses, and also qualities. The slates have a high reputation; they have been in use for many decades throughout the world, from Argentina to Australia.

Architects and builders acknowledge the value of the slate. Consequently, Llechwedd craftsmen are fully occupied in creating hearths made of solid slate – slates which are both durable and attractive, window cills which do not deteriorate and which defy the vagaries of the weather, mantelpieces which are well-designed and strong. Slates in a wide variation of colours, taken from these mines, are fashioned into patio flooring, which has the advantage of being warm in winter and cool in summer, and also crazy paving which is artistic in colouring and lasting. The building industry also recognises the worth of the slate for cladding, because of its versatility and moisture-resistant qualities.

The slate quarries of Wales are justly famed. The largest slate-producing areas in the worldwere those in North-East Wales. They have a magnetic appeal to tourists, especially now that there are opportunities for travelling in the subterranean caverns. The Dinorwic Quarries cover nine hundred acres. West of Snowdon, near Nantlle lies the Cilgwyn Quarry, the oldest in the neighbourhood. Important quarries were situated around Blaenau Ffestiniog, Corwen, Corris and Abergynolwyn. The Presceli Mountain area in South-West Wales has also yielded a rich harvest of slate.

The interest of the Romans in Welsh gold is often mentioned. It may well be conjectured that they were also keenly interested in Welsh slates, for they used them as roofing material. Up to the close of the eighteenth century slate workings in Wales were extremely crude. An impetus was given to the slate industry in the nineteenth century by the boom in building. The industry suffered vicissitudes following the economic repercussions of two world wars. Today, the demand for slate is small, compared to heretofore.

Skilled workers are essential in the slate industry to work on the great slate beds, sometimes on the surface, sometimes underground. Much of the finer work has to be done by hand. Thus emerges the true craftsman who takes a personal pride in his work. Miss Dorothy Hartley has paid a fine tribute to the character of the true born rockman. He has, she says, 'a farmer's patience, a woodman's imagination, and the constructive vision and balanced mind of the mathematician'. The rockman, she says, will arrive at an equation demanding mathematical formulae beyond his conscious calculation. Moreover in days of old he could do this and other wonderful things, though perhaps he had not the skill wherewith to read.

Slate is comparatively soft and is a metamorphic rock of great age. The Welsh slate is classed as Ordovician, or of Lower Silurian Age, and during its formative processes it was subject to tremendous natural pressure and intense heat. The thickness of the slate deposits varies from 150 to as much as 300 feet. Beds of chert and other rocks of a harder nature are inter-stratified within the slate beds. The beds of slate are classified and are named – the New Vein, the Old Vein, the Back or Middle Vein, and the North Vein. The colours of the slates vary. Those of Blaenau Ffestiniog are a soft blue-grey; those of Dinorwic offer a greater range of colour – blue, grey, red and sea-green. Today, by modern processes, the slates can be coloured into rich or pastel shades by treatment, which adds to the beauty of the material, and which is beneficial to the slates.

In the nineteenth century there was a universal demand for roofing slates. They were also used for building. Large slates were required for partitioning, for steps, for floors, and for lintels. Heavy slates, larger than those used for roofing, were often hung as protection on the leeward side of a mountain homestead or cottage. Within the dairy, the farm wife acknowledged freely the value of slate, recognising its cooling qualities. She insisted that her slab table, her sink, her shelves should be of slate. Invaluable too in the days before the advent of the mechanical separator, was the *sleten*, the finely cut wisp of slate of cobweb fineness which she used to gather the cream from the bowls of milk. Such is the traditional prestige of the *sleten*, that many a skilled dairywoman will, to this day, revert to its use when she wants to make a special supply of butter.

The use of slate in building generally, and as a roofing material, is reviving. Its advantages for roofing are many. Slates are more enduring than thatch or tiles, lasting intact for a century or more when properly nailed. Because of this, lightweight slate is economic in use. Slate is water-tight and fireproof, and its thermal conductivity is low. It does not corrode from acids, neither does it harbour vegetation or vermin.

An important feature of slate is its subjection to cleavage. Unlike most other rocks, it is entirely independent of its original bedding. From a strip of slate one and a quarter inches thick, a skilled quarryman can cut as many as 26 strips. Furthermore, these fine strips can be bent in an arc. For practical purposes, however, the quarryman seldom cuts the slates to a thickness less than one-sixth of an inch. It is estimated that Welsh slate has a tensile strength of 8,470 lbs per square inch, and a resistance to compression of 31,431 lbs per square inch.

Slate knapping is a skilled and specialised craft, and the dexterity entailed is recognised by the Welsh communities which delight in watching competitions in the art. These tournaments of craftsmanship are features of country shows and sheepdog trials. Even a cynical observer is enthralled by the skill which the quarrymen show in splitting the delicate slates to hair-breadth thicknesses. Surety of touch, allied to well-balanced tools, used with astonishing accuracy and speed, result in the cutting-up of the slates to the most exacting measurements. Great skill is required in cleaning and dressing the slates; it is done with thin broad wedges and wooden mallets.

Roofing slates were given particular names according to their sizes. Units, doubles and headers are some of their names; then, by a peculiar form of nomenclature, there is a female hierarchy. *Ladies* were slates which were narrow and small; then came viscountesses, countesses, queens and empresses. In these more standardised days the names are falling into disuse.

It was usual to sell the slates by the thousand; the 'long' thousand being 1,260 slates.

Building contractors seek supplies of Welsh slate for the manufacture of brewery tanks, and for billiard, dairy and laboratory tables. There is a demand for it for monumental work, and for aquaria. The aquarium at the London Zoo is built of Welsh slate.

SLATE MEMORIAL STONES

An interesting use of slate was made by monumental masons. The old church and chapel yards of Wales retain numbers of slate headstones. Within the churches and chapels, too, there are numerous memorial tablets of slate, testifying to a vernacular art in a more vigorous manner, for they have been protected from the rigours of the weather. Many of the slate memorial stones date from the late seventeenth century. By the end of the eighteenth century, while retaining much of their original vigour and charm, they lost something of their social status, appearing, despite the high pedigree of birth inscribed on some of them, as poor relations of some of the more ornate granite and marble memorials, which represent a later trade and fashion.

The skill of the monumental masons of the time is evident on the slate memorials of the seventeenth and eighteenth centuries. Lettering is in Welsh (sometimes painfully Anglicised), in English and in Latin. It is usually incised into the slate, whether the memorial is for outside or for inside erection. Motifs, forming decoration, are usually placed at the top or bottom of the inscription; sometimes they form a border right around the whole.

Among the motifs which usually appear are cherubs (sometimes blowing trumpets), skeletons, flowers – particularly daisies, garlands of flowers and of leaves, the whole being enclosed in scroll work in the rococo manner. The predominance of the same motifs arranged in a uniform style within a locality, suggests that the existence of some particular stone mason or family of craftsmen.

Such a family was that of Brute, whose memorial stones may still be seen in the southern districts of the Welsh Marches in South-East Wales, in Herefordshire, and in areas of Black Mountain moorland, well away from the slate quarry regions. The work of this family of stone masons dates from the early eighteenth century until about 1850.

The Brute family used a naïve decoration on their slate slabs in the form of a colouring obtained from vegetable dyes. In many crafts, secret skills are preserved jealously within a family freemasonry. The Brute family had a special method of obtaining dyes from vegetables and lichens. This precious formula they inscribed in a family Bible. Unfortunately for craftsmanship, the Bible was lost about 1850, and a further disaster was that no one of the Brute family knew the process.

The decoration was done in yellow, blue, red and green; gilding was often introduced. A thick black paint was sometimes used for economy, taking the place of incised work. It is remarkable that the brilliant colours have been preserved so well.

The fashion in slate memorials was for plain, rectangular slabs. These were set up as headstones or fastened to the walls of churches. Pediments and aprons were attached to the more elaborate memorials. When a vogue arose for oval shapes, highly decorated, the country stone mason, realising the peculiarities of his materials, wisely remained conservative and confined himself to mural tablets of rectangular form. The finest collection of tablets made by the Brute family is at Llangattock Church. Here there are nine mural tablets arranged in three rows on the vestry walls. The Brute masons remained impervious to the classical revival. While some of their contemporaries, such as the Hereford masons, John Pritchard and Thomas Roberts of Longtown, were creating elaborate stones, incised with copperplate writing, the Brute masons retained their preference for the baroque.

A memorial at Llanbedr Church is of stone, not slate. It reads:

'In memory of Thomas, ye son of Thomas Brute, *vide* Mason, who died ye 5th Day of February A.D. 1724. Aged 2 years 10 months. Vivit post funera virtus Mors Janua Vitae.'

The material, *stone*, shows that the Brute masons worked in material other than slate. In view of the personal attachment to the little tablet, the decoration may well be taken to represent the height of the craftsman's art. The motifs are symbolised to a high degree; colouring was introduced on to the cherub head with folded wings and on palm leaves, wreaths and flowers.

Brute fecit, inscribed upon slate or stone, may be compared to other family names inscribed, generation after generation within the craft, and localised within an area, e.g. the Williams stonemason family of Llandeilo, Dyfed. On slate and on stone, such craftsmen have fostered as well as created a particular form of decoration within their vicinity, as assuredly as other craftsmen have worked in wood or in metal.

The worker in stone, loving his material, loving his craft, plied his skill, independent and indifferent to the social changes which swept away aristocratic patronage, and which introduced many vagaries of taste. They remained true to their tradition, seeing that slate and local stone harmonised with the Welsh landscape; they refused to pay allegiance to the standardised memorial stones, and the more stereotyped designs which were mass-produced.

Many memorial slabs were enhanced with paint and with gilding. The brilliant colouring of the Brute tablets has defied the onslaughts of time. In the *Architectural Review*, October 1947, there is an account of the Brute memorial stones. An interesting suggestion is put forward that the name Brute may have been derived by way of

Brutus and Brut from the sixteenth-century variant, which referred to a man of Celtic or Welsh descent as opposed to a man of Anglo-Saxon or Danish lineage.

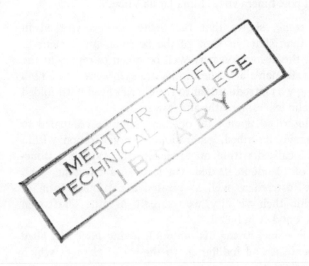

— 4 —
Woodcraft

THE SPOON CARVER

DAN THEOPHILUS, Y NADDWR LLWYAU

Grahame Amey is a maker of furniture. In 1969 he entered on an enterprise which has proved remarkably successful. He took over a fifteenth-century semi-derelict granary at Crickhowell, between Abergavenny and Brecon, and renovated it into a workshop. There, with his partner Jonathan Beagley, he makes high-class furniture of a high standard of craftsmanship, largely designed by himself. The furniture is simple and elegant, and much of it is exported to America, Canada and Australia. Five craftsmen are employed. Four of these have served their apprenticeship in the workshop. Each piece of furniture is made by one man. His particular stamp is shown on the article of furniture, as well as the nameplate of Grahame Amey Limited. An individual craftsman chooses his own wood, and undertakes all the processes to the final polishing and dusting. He is able to do things in the way he particularly likes. He uses first-class materials, and designs which are simple but elegant. Most of the furniture made on the premises is in corn-blond ash and oak. Solid timber is used throughout. Screws are of brass. A finish is given with a heat- and stain-resistant polish, which is then hand-waxed.

A form of industrial democracy is practised, and the craftsman can earn a bonus for working quickly. Finished articles are judged by a committee.

Costing is affected by the exigencies of labour. The furniture, which is displayed in the showroom, is not cheap, but it represents work that will endure for more than one generation. Furniture made by Grahame Amey Ltd will be the antiques of future years.

Woodcrafts of Clwyd. This is a family firm producing fine quality work for their displays at Colwyn Bay, Clwyd. The workshop is at Dyserth, near Rhyl.

The firm concentrates on work in established styles. The use of power tools is at a minimum : the emphasis is always on handwork. Mr Owen C. Owen specialises in the making of furniture. He also creates toys; mainly large trains and rocking horses. He uses solid timber of mahogany and teak. The finished article is oiled to bring out the true grain and characteristics of the timber.

Mr William Owen, a versatile worker, delights in turnery. He works to his own designs, the tools being chisels. Using a wooden lathe he turns articles from small egg cups to pedestal ash trays. Woodcrafts of Clwyd in their display room give prominence to the work of other craftsmen also. Handicraft materials, both retail and wholesale, are sold to skilled craftsmen, as well as to encourage amateurs.

Philip Wilson of Harlech is a furniture maker. With the happy and sympathetic co-operation of his wife, Isobel, who herself takes a practical interest in crafts, he embarked on his venture in Harlech, following on an earlier enterprise at Winchcombe in Gloucestershire.

Philip Wilson works entirely on his own. He is responsible for every stage in making the furniture, from designing to finishing. He uses machines for some of the routine work, for cutting and joints. Even so, much of the shaping is done by hand, especially for the details such as chamfers, etc., which most manufacturers today consider to be uneconomic.

Philip Wilson gives priority to Welsh oak. This he seasons himself. Every piece is made individually, whether to a customer's requirements, or to his own design. He avoids creating work which is startlingly modern, and also 'reproduction antique' work. He aims at combining traditional and contemporary elements, and also at blending solidity with grace. His preference is for unstained wood.

A dining room suite in the Wilson showroom has proved to have special appeal. The refectory table is late Gothic in feeling; there is an unusual treatment of the framework and legs. The chairs have rush seats. Orders for this suite are very numerous; they involve work lasting several years.

Smaller items are also made in the workshops. These include lamp bases and carved dishes, individually shaped and made from a variety of woods. Abstract wood sculptures are created from driftwood, or from new timber.

Handel Edwards of Skewen, Swansea is a skilled wood carver. Following on an apprenticeship in the building industry, he devoted himself to carving in wood. He achieved mastery, and is now acclaimed as a superb artist-craftsman. He has had the loyal and happy co-operation of his wife in his enterprises, and he has had a remarkably long list of successes.

At first he carved in mahogany with heavy carpentry tools. He carved a face, and with such success that he was inspired to go further. He disciplined himself to study; he practised and learnt by trial and error, and now he carves fine pieces in the studio-workshop in his garden. The carved pieces are the strongest evidence of his remarkable skill, and total dedication to his craft.

There is in his home a carved scene from Charles Dickens' *Oliver Twist*. Every character is depicted. Another realistic relief carving has been shown in many exhibitions. It measures five feet by three feet. It is carved in mahogany, and portrays a kitchen in a miner's home in Wales. The miner is having a bath in a tin tub before the fire. Introduced into the same carving is an underground scene. Miners in different occupations are depicted.

Handel Edwards is a versatile craftsman. His carvings cover a wide range of subjects. They are marked by their fine artistry, skilful carving and exquisite detail.

The Welsh Arts Council has recognised the value of his work. He can now undertake commissions.

FURNITURE MAKERS

In the main these work in solid wood; oak, beech, yew, elm and pine. Styles vary, and include the traditional, modern, and cottage types. Some specialise in farmhouse furniture, others in furniture suitable for churches, chapels, public buildings and also public houses. Up-to-date designs are allied to traditional proportions and fine craftsmanship, assuring durability. Some furniture makers undertake antique restoration and repairs, including re-upholstery, and repolishing. Gilding, carving and marquetry are practised in some of the more specialist craft workshops.

Allied to the making of furniture proper, a worker in wood may create such articles as bread- and cheese-boards, table lamps, and hand-turned wood bowls and musical boxes. Some make a speciality of clocks long-case clocks, grandfather and grandmother clocks, and wall clocks and barometers. The clocks have eight-day spring- or battery-driven movements.

The country carpenter has been an essential craftsman in the community since man began to build. His work has allied itself naturally with that of the mason and blacksmith. In wooded areas he is often identified with the country builder. In the Severn Valley for instance, it was he, in the main, who constructed the timber-frame houses, filling in the spaces between the oak timbering with wattle and wash and, in later times, with brick nogging. Until the close of the fifteenth century, the worker in wood created dwellings for men and for beasts. Even when stone was available, the carpenter was still essential for making doors, windows, and floors. Farm buildings, the equipping of stable, byre and stye, called for the ingenuity of the carpenter. He may have lacked the techniques of modern agricultural planners, but he had practical understanding of the requirements of the animals and the comfort of the farmer, as he worked among them. He planned and built with a practical man's appreciation of space, realising how animals love to sprawl. His lay-out took into consideration matters such as drainage, and he worked with an eye to the natural characteristics of the land. He worked to co-operate with the farmer, and called in the stone mason to provide him with the stones on which to rest his construction in successful defiance of the farmer's enemy, the rat.

Such a craftsman as the carpenter, ingenious and co-operative, would be essential even in the early communities. As soon as Man had subjected iron to his use, the metal was enlisted for the carpenter's tools. These were few at first, but in dextrous hands they were capable of performing versatile work. In the old Welsh laws, though the carpenter appears to have ranked lower in the scale than the blacksmith, nevertheless, his position was high. The possibility that most peasants, once in possession of some carpenter's tools, assayed work upon wood, may have, in some measure, detracted from the specialised nature of the craft. Yet there were branches of woodwork which demanded the intricate skill of the carpenter himself, and the presence of numerous lay-workers probably helped rather than opposed him in an age when he was over-burdened with demands of work.

A hierarchy of craftsmen grew up within the craft itself, partly due to the ordinances of Norman law, which classified carpenters into those who worked for the King, for the Church, and for the populace. Royal carpenters were essentially specialists; they were *directors* who enlisted humbler carpenters to carry out their plans. Carpenters who worked in Church and Monastery have left abundant examples of their skilled craftsmanship. Old records prove that they were well provided for. More telling is the workmanship which they bequeathed; only a craftsman happy within himself could have created such fine specimens of woodwork, evidence that they were labours of love. The country carpenter's conditions were less favourable. He faced long hours and continuous demands on his skill, but he experienced the craftsman's joy of creation and derived pleasure from the knowledge that he was essential in the lives of his fellow men.

Changes in social and economic life and the vicissitudes of agriculture had their effect on the craft. Formal education widened, and the older craftsmen encouraged their sons to enter other spheres.

The modern carpenter has introduced up-to-date equipment into his workshop. He values it as an ally against the slowness of certain manual processes. Further, the harnessing of electricity has extended his range of work.

TYPES OF FURNITURE

A tradition of fine craftsmanship in furniture-making existed in Wales, down to the coming of machinery with the Industrial Revolution. Commercialism then crept into the crafts, and hand labour gave place to the tending of a machine. Interest in design was divorced from craftsmanship, and a man no longer took a personal pride in the product he was creating, nor did he have any personal knowledge of the customer whose wants he was purporting to satisfy. Thus ended the long and noble tradition of furniture-making in Wales.

The earliest makers of furniture were probably not specialists in the work. A farmer would fell the trees on his land and endeavour to make a chest or table to fill a need within his home. As the carpenter emerged as a craftsman in the community, he may have tended to set a fashion in style, improving on the rough work more generally accepted in a locality. The earlier work reflects primitiveness and paucity of tools. Planks were riven not sawn, and were finished with the aid of an adze only. The smith may have assisted by embellishing such work. He provided strong nails, such as have defied rust for centuries, and he gave simple but pleasing adornment to chests and cupboards with strengthening bands of metals, curved and foliated at their ends.

The *chest* was one of the earliest forms of furniture, and in some form or other it was found in most buildings in Wales, both ecclesiastical and secular. Great chests of dark oak wood stood in the monasteries and churches, holding vestments and treasures of money and plate. Smaller chests served from one generation to another in the stately homes of landowners, and in the cottages of the peasantry, holding valuables, clothing and grain. A dower chest, beautifully carved, was a personal treasure. Oak chests were usual, but other woods also were used. A chest lined with cedar was valued, as the wood was impervious to moth.

The chest proper evolved with the centuries into the *tall boy*, a chest of drawers fixed upon another chest of drawers. A *mule chest* had two small drawers beneath it. Known as *y coffer bach* and the *Welsh Bible box*, it is a type of its own. Oak or elm were the usual woods used. Holly was introduced for inlaid work. A name or verse was sometimes carved on the front panel. A Bible, a rare and precious possession, was kept within the small chest, and family and legal papers were stored in the small drawer below.

A special form of chest was known as a *coffer*. Some were tithe chests; others were used to store corn. Some had half-rounded lids to amplify storage space.

The chest provided a box seat. Some ingenious furniture-maker conceived the idea of fitting it with a back, and later, with sides. The high-backed *settle* which thus emerged proved most suitable for use in the kitchen of a cottage, farmhouse or inn. To its sociable nature was added the advantage of a draught excluder, while the deep box seat was an admirable receptacle for storage. The austerity of the oak or elm seat was sometimes softened by the addition of a down cushion provided from the farm or inn yard.

Chairs developed from the box seat. Benches were for long familiar in Welsh houses, chairs being, as late as the seventeeth century, the perquisites of the rich. With time, box-like chairs assumed a more graceful form; they grew lighter and had straight panelled backs. The legs were made longer and were fitted with stretchers.

Styles in *tables* changed with the years. Trestle tables which could be removed with ease were usual in cottage and hall. Solid tables came into use. Legs were fitted permanently into the ends, and stretchers strengthened them.

The *cupboard* was an essential article of furniture. The *cwpwrdd deuddarn* was familiar in the sixteenth century. Sometimes it took the form of a *cwpwrdd tridarn*, a three-sectional cupboard. These cupboards were used for storage, and for the display of silver, pewter and silverware. Later these cupboards were fitted with glass doors.

The furniture-maker also made *beds*. It was he who provided a wooden cradle. This became a family heirloom. The wooden box-bed fitted into the wall had warmth and cosiness, but it was abandoned in the interests of health and hygiene. Bedsteads came into use. The truckle bed was a subsidiary bedstead, which could be pushed under a main bedstead when not in use. Mattresses were corded into these, and they were used by servants and children. Tester or tent beds had elaborate carvings and 'barley twist' ornamental pillars which served to set off the rich curtains.

The homely nature of his work led the country furniture-maker to remain faithful to his native woods, such as oak and elm. Sometimes he used beech, ash, holly, apple and yew. The individual craftsman created his own idiosyncracies and patterns.

For long the tradition of simple furniture-making in Wales survived the onslaught of the forces of the Industrial Revolution, and a fair amount of individual work was carried on.

A gallant attempt was made in the 1930's to establish the craft of furniture-making at Brynmawr in Gwent. The venture had its inspiration from Peter Scott. The craftsmen, inspired by designer Paul Matt, produced furniture in fine design. This found a ready and discriminating market until the close of the venture at the outbreak of World War II.

Today, state-sponsored organisations are ready to assist and guide the furniture-maker in his efforts to obtain suitable and well-seasoned hardwoods, especially oak, beech and walnut, and to give him practical help in the creation and marketing of fine work.

The Woodworker's Ballad

All this is moulded in iron,
Has lent to destruction and blood;
But the things that are honoured of Zion,
Are most of them made of wood.

Stone can be chiselled to beauty,
And iron shines bright for defence,
But when Mother Earth pondered her duty,
She brought forth the forest from whence—

Come tables and chairs and crosses,
Little things that a hot iron warps,
Old ships that the blue wave tosses,
And fiddles for music, and harps.

King Arthur had a wood table
And our Lord blessed wood, for you see
He was born in a wooden stable,
And died on a wooden tree.

And he sailed in a wooden vessel
On the waters of Galilee,
And he worked on a wooden table
At his wonderful carpentry.

Oh! all that is moulded of iron
Has led to destruction and blood;
But the things that are honoured of Zion
Are most of them made of wood.

THE TOOL-MAKER

The turner often made tool handles working in conjunction with the blacksmith. He made handles for axe-heads and shovels. At times he worked independently, making hay rakes entirely of wood.

Specialised skill goes into the making of such tools for they must be light in handling and yet strong in use. The nature of the land on which the tools are to be used is also a consideration with a good craftsman. When he creates rakes he bears in mind whether they are needed for use on lush grassland, or on the short grass of the steeper Welsh hillside.

A good craftsman will also consider the tool in actual use. He sets full value on sound balance, on the sharpness of the tines which must be set at the correct angle in the rake head. Not only must the handles be smooth, but they must be of the correct length.

The steaming of tool handles has fallen into disuse with the coming of rotary cutting machines. The better rakes are made from hand-cleft wood, usually elm. A clogger's knife is used to sharpen the teeth. The value and service of hand-cleft handles remain unchallenged.

TURNERY AND CARVING

Ken Jones of Llanarth, Cardigan, has high qualifications in mechanical engineering. He opted out of industry, and he has made a remarkable success as a carver of love spoons. His order books are full of requests from all parts of Britain. His spoons are much in evidence throughout craft shops in Wales. Further success followed his exhibition at the Welsh Craft Fair at Llandrindod Wells, and he exports his love spoons to America, Australia and Canada. With the co-operation of his brothers, he is now contemplating converting premises in Aberaeron, Ceredigion into a craft shop. There his love spoons will be given special prominence.

The wooden spoon was a familiar sight in Welsh kitchens, along with other table-ware made in the same medium. Their use dates back to mediaeval times.

The Love Spoon had a romantic and decorative association. A young man would carve a love spoon and present it to his young lady as a token of his affection.

With time, the functional purpose of such a spoon became less and less apparent. The handle was enlarged and carved and decorated. The intricate designs and carvings were manifestly a labour of love. The amateur, with the skilled carver, spent the long winter evenings in creating a spoon fully worthy of presentation.

By tradition, a true love spoon was carved from one piece of wood. The tools used were simple and primitive. Considerable skill went into the work.

It was usual for the handle to carry a panel of wood. This served as a vehicle for intricate carving. The symbols carved had their own individual meaning; hearts bearing initials, hearts intertwined, heraldic shields. A heart denoted the young man's love for the recipient. A key hole implied that he was prepared to set up house for her. A wheel indicated his preparedness to work for her. A chain fashioned from the wood carried several links. These showed the number of children the lover desired. The spoon itself symbolised his hope to provide for her. Two bowls fitted to one handle indicated constancy and unity.

A young lady was free to accept several spoons – and even retain those from admirers whom she rejected.

The custom of presenting love spoons continued to the close of the nineteenth century.

Love spoons are still being carved. They are often presented on ceremonial occasions as traditional tokens from Wales.

Men still delight in carving love spoons. Indeed, competitions in the art are held from time to time.

The continuity of craftsmanship is at times strikingly apparent, and turnery, like pottery, can be classified among the most ancient of crafts. How deeply rooted are certain crafts in the racial life of the people! Men of the Stone Age were the parents of many of the crafts in Wales. It is significant of their ingenuity, when we consider turnery, that they fashioned adzes, saws and drills out of flint long before the use of metal was discovered. The primitive method employed by the Red Indians to kindle a fire by friction, or for boring a hole in some surface, is by the use of a bow drill. The upper end of a rod or drill inserted in a piece of wood is held in the teeth, and the drill is twisted by a thong of hide, the ends of which are held in the teeth. On much the same principle, a pole lathe was used for turning wood by primitive people long before they fashioned metal into their service.

The use of the pole lathe appears to have been common to most countries of Europe. Dr Iorwerth Peate in *Y Crefftwr Yng Nghymru* has elucidated the culture of the people of the Lake Settlements of Britain, and has told how among their remains have been discovered examples of turnery excellent in their craftsmanship and in their design. Most of the work created by modern turners bears a very close affinity with that made in Europe in pre-Christian days.

The turner was known in Wales as *Y Saer Gwyn*. He worked in white wood. Sycamore, alder and ash are now used, the latter being used extensively in more recent times for the fashioning of tool handles by means of automatic lathes. Beechwood is used by chair bodgers for chair legs; beech is made into a variety of articles useful in the shoe trade, such as shoe heels and lasts; it is also used for platters, bowls and domestic ware. In the seventeenth and eighteenth centuries, the pole-lathe turner made spoons and dishes of an ornamental character. Work of the latter type was sometimes made from the wood of the wild cherry. Articles were bored and pierced. The wood resembled mahogany, and its rich red brown shadings were sometimes enhanced by soaking in lime water. The sweet fragrance of the wood added to the charm.

Before the introduction of ceramics, of enamel and tin-plate ware, wooden utensils were used extensively in Welsh homes. Their simple designs had a hygienic value, and constant scourings in cold water safeguarded them against unpleasant aromas. Wooden bowls, trenchers and platters graced the shelves of the kitchen dresser. Spoons were given a special rack. Many a young woman received such a rack bearing her name, as a love token from her sweetheart.

Spoons of different capacity were made, ranging from the tiny spoon that would fit into a small salt cellar to a massive dipper that could scoop up the pig swill. Functionalism gave to these spoons a strong and simple beauty, greater than any which could be achieved by extraneous ornament. The spurtle or oatmeal porridge spoon, had a pointed handle (useful sometimes as a surface poker of the coals!) and a bowl that was flattened at the edge to enable the cook to scrape up the gruel. Other spoons had a hook at the end of the handle. This was useful for hanging the spoon on the edge of the pot in the process of cooking. The hook varied in size according to the bowl of the spoon. Squared, and made the same depth as the bowl, it formed a little stand when placed upon the table.

Spoons became in the hands of amateur turners elaborate affairs, vehicles of carving and sentiment. The functional value of the spoon diminished. The handle was lengthened beyond any utilitarian purpose; it was broadened and pierced and carved and embellished with a motto, or the name of some young lady. Sometimes a wooden chain, cunningly carved, was affixed to the end of the handle. Of course, such spoons were not meant for use; they were frankly love tokens. The term 'spooning', meaning 'amorous', is said to derive from the custom of giving such spoons as love tokens.

Turners also made very fine drawing and skimming spoons for skimming the surface of the cream from bowls of milk. Great skill was required to make this delicate spoon of a light and almost transparent nature. Such spoons, as well as the more elaborate love tokens, were often objects of competition in local eisteddfodau. The functional worth of the skimming spoon made it a worthy object of popular attention, a characteristic wholly lacking in the craftsmanship of the carved spoons which rendered them at times grotesque.

Wooden platters of varying sizes were made by the turner, and also wooden bowls. With remarkable skill a turner would carve a nest of bowls from one block of wood. He fashioned many articles for domestic use. A housewife might receive as a token of regard a rack of rolling pins. Three or more rolling pins rested one above the other on a small notched rack. Their surfaces were of different kinds according to their use. A grooved rolling pin was used to crush thin oatcakes into small pieces; one with a knobbly surface was used to crush oaten bread for broth. One rolling pin was smooth for rolling pastry. Butter hands and butter stamps were the speciality of the skilled turner, along with wooden moulds that shaped the butter into pound sizes. Imagination was linked with skill in the designing of the butter prints, which became the unofficial copyright of the farm that bought them. A spray of heather, or pine trees, against a skyline, might be, by the turner's decision, the insignia of a hill croft, whereas a swan gliding on the river or a cow grazing in a meadow might be the device of a valley farm.

The turner's hand was much in evidence in the dairy. He made milking stools. The rounded stools are often grooved in a manner peculiar to a certain locality, and the depth of the seat is characteristic of certain areas. Three-cornered stools are favoured in certain districts, one corner being softly rounded. Some stools have square seats; some have three legs, and some four. Some have a low squared back.

The hand turner concentrates on the making of round and semi-round articles. Even so, his range is wide. When engaged on solid turning he uses his chisel on the surface of the revolving wood and inserts the curved blade of a knife on the inner side. By this method he can make bowls with comparative rapidity.

When making tool handles or chair legs he employs solid turning, chiselling only on the convex surface of the wood. Semi-rounded articles are made by cutting a rounded article transversely, a method employed in the making of broom heads.

In the Wye Valley arose turneries making full use of water power. A plentiful supply of timber was ensured from the woods at Tintern. Where there was sufficient power from a water-wheel to drive several lathes, workmen would congregate in a small workshop and co-operate in a simple factory organisation. Where there were treadle lathes, foot pressure was used, and a crank fitted to the lathe ensured a continuous rotary movement.

Richly wooded areas in the Usk and Wye Valleys provide many deciduous trees useful to turners. Consequently, in localities of the Forest of Dean, and South-Eastern Gwent and Powys, turners used the available material to turn chair legs. They worked their lathes either in the woods or small workshops. True craftsmanship is clearly apparent in the turning of a chair leg. The worker – the chair bodger – does not use the seemingly convenient rounded branches growing in a wood. He hews out a rectangular block of wood. He eschews the rounded branch for he is aware of the hidden knots, the uneven shrinking, the soft inner core. He concentrates on his solid block.

In Wales it is usual to see a turner stand at his work. He works at a bench which stands at a height of about four feet from the ground. Some think that the pole lathe was in universal use because of the dearth of water power. In contradiction to this there is a strong tradition of turnery in South-Western Wales, especially in the Teifi Valley, areas where water power could be harnessed with apparent ease. The turner, dependent on sycamore and alder trees – great lovers of water – tended to settle in areas where these trees flourished.

The pole lathe, the oldest device in turning, consists of a horizontal rod, supported at one end, and in the middle, by wooden uprights. Rotation on this rod lies between a bent sapling above and a treadle beneath. A narrow leather strap is wound around the horizontal rod. The end of the strap is fashioned to a treadle placed on the ground. Pressure on the treadle ensures that the rod turns towards the worker; releasing of pressure makes the rod turn in the opposite way. Thus is achieved the rotary motion of an article, which is subjected to the turner's chisel. The turner applies this tool on the forward stroke, and withdraws it, as the rod turns in the opposite direction.

A simple pole lathe of this nature could be fashioned by the actual worker. He sometimes introduced some minor innovations in the general pattern. The uprights, or poppets, were adjustable along the bed of the lathe. In this way rods of varying lengths could be turned. When turning bowls the turner would sometimes fix them to another rod called a chunk. A strap wound around this ensured rotation.

The Teifi Valley on the confines of North Pembrokeshire and South Cardiganshire has been renowned for sycamore trees since the days of the Mabinogion. In this region the use of the pole lathe persisted; pole-lathe turners fashioned wooden spoons, bowls, egg cups, platters and other articles of domestic use. Sycamore is a favourite wood for it is not only plentiful, but it does not affect the taste or the colour of food. Apple wood is sometimes used, and oak is sometimes favoured for tool handles.

CLOG-MAKING

A revived vogue in the wearing of clogs has given a new impetus to a declining craft. The enterprise of a young clog-maker, *Hywel Davies of Chapel Street, Tregaron*, in the heart of Ceredigion, is proving successful. Demands for clogs have been steady from fashion-conscious wearers and for children, as well as from agricultural workers. The development of a more European way of life has also increased the demand.

Hywel Davies uses hand-made soles shaped from local timber. The range of styles is wide, varying from the open Scandinavian type to the old traditional Welsh patterns.

The vicissitudes of fashion have naturally affected the clog trade. For centuries clogs were worn universally in most parts of Wales. Then, from the time of World War I, the wearing of clogs, and consequently the making of clogs, declined. During World War II there was a revival in the wearing of clogs, for shoes and boots were rationed and difficult to obtain.

With the growth in popularity, clog-makers, fewer in number

than before, in order to meet the pressure of demand, found them-selves obliged to use factory machine-made soles from Yorkshire. Not many seem to have returned to the craft of making their own soles.

Few versatile clog-makers were left in Wales. Solitary clog-makers were to be found in such places as Llanpumpsaint, Cynwyl Elfed and Cardigan in Dyfed, and also Wrexham in Clwyd. These used bought-in soles and uppers catering for a restricted, and only partly traditional, market.

At Tregaron, Hywel Davies uses hand-made soles. They are made of local timber. He has the advantage of having been trained by a veteran clog-maker, Mr Henry Davies of Llanpumpsaint, Dyfed.

The use of the clogger's knife calls for skill. The knife is peculiar to the craft, and expertise in handling it comes with experience. The blade is about six inches long and four inches wide. To it is attached a long handle which allows for considerable leverage, for the blade is attached by a small hook to a wooden block. The clog-maker uses the knife with a levering motion of his right hand, and holds the clog-block with his left hand. The block is set on the ground, and he has to bend low over his work. The movements of his blade call for considerable precision.

The legend has flourished – and was fostered among older clog-gers – that one had to learn the craft in boyhood to obtain mastery on the clogger's knife. The clog-maker learns to lever his hand automatically on the handle; his eye is concentrated on the clog-block.

The clogger uses a sharp knife in making the soles. He trims each sole roughly and then pairs them. Next, he takes the sharp knife around the edges and shapes the instep. As the clog sole does not bend the spring is given by *shaping*, and by achieving the right thickness at the ball of the foot.

Clog-making is an ancient craft which has long graced the Welsh woodlands. In times past it was carried on as a separate occupation. Later it became associated with that of the village cobbler.

Clog-making belongs to the under-wood crafts. The main timber of the woodlands was used by the carpenter and wheelwright. Smallwood remained, giving supplies to the woodland craftsmen. Certain trees were cultivated for smallwood. The main stems of young saplings were pruned, causing side buds to sprout. Wood

thus treated formed a copse. Many species of trees were treated in
this way.

Clogs were worn extensively in Wales over a long period. The
clog differs from the French *sabot*, which is made entirely of wood,
in that it has a coarse leather upper, much the same as the pattern
of a boot or shoe. Usually the clog has an iron strip attached around
the sole and heel formation; a metal toecap protects the front from
wear. Pattens, or flat rings, were fitted on the soles when used for
walking over wet ground, or uneven surfaces such as cobblestones.
A puckling clog had a sharp metal point reminiscent of a bayonet;
such footwear was particularly formidable in a scrimmage.

In Wales cloggers have often worked in small bands, camping in
the woods and travelling from one estate to another in search of
the required smallwood. Clogs were made to meet local needs, and
to meet the demands of Lancashire employers, who required clogs
of the alder which was plentiful in Wales. Clogging was often a
family concern. A boy became an unofficial apprentice to his father.
Six or seven cloggers would travel the woodlands, working as an
independent band. The main rivals of these bands were the gypsies,
themselves adept at clog-making and who often entered into con-
tract work.

Bands of cloggers journeyed in the valleys of the Severn and
Wye, and along smaller rivers such as the Usk. Away from the
Welsh border they worked in more isolated groups and in more
remote places. The south-western valleys of Wales, with their heavy
rainfall, were ideal grounds for the growing of alder and sycamore.
South Cardiganshire and Pembrokeshire had many cloggers.

Alder and sycamore were considered the best materials, but
birchwood and willow were also used. Alder is coarse-grained, and
the wood is therefore soft; because of this, however, its durability
is less. Its absorbing qualities lessens its worth for wear in damp
places. The alder trees are usually cut at about 25 years growth,
when the trunk is about nine or ten inches in diameter. The trees
can only be cut in spring and summer, and the clog soles must be
stacked for a period for drying.

Some cloggers concentrated, not on the making of soles, but in
the cutting of wood to supply machines that made soles. Beechwood and birch were often used for mass-produced clog soles. They
are inferior woods, despite their coarse grain and imperviousness
to moisture.

BOAT BUILDING

Interest in boat building must have existed in Wales in early times. It was by sea that Welshmen maintained connection with Ireland, and with the northern countries of Europe.

Boats of the galley type are known to have been used. In the fourteenth century there are records of the building and repairing of ships in Swansea, Cardiff and Carmarthen.

In the Middle Ages Welsh vessels were numbered among the King's fleet. The carrying trade grew in importance, as the wine, salt, fruit and iron of Spain were exchanged for Welsh wool, cloth and hides. Wine was conveyed from Plymouth to Conway, and from Doncaster to Beaumaris.

The names of several Welsh ships have been preserved. D. Thomas in *Hen Longau a Llongwyr Cymru* refers to *Coga Sanctie Marie* (St. Mary's Boat) of Conway; *Seinte Marie Cogge* of Pembroke; *Cogge John* of Kidwelly; *Le Spaynnol* of Haverfordwest; *Julian de Kermerdyn* of Carmarthen; the *Trinity* of Tenby; the *Lydnart* of Cardigan.

Wales was caught up in the seaward expansion of the Tudor dynasty. Schooled among the currents of the rough Bristol Channel and of the Irish Seas, Welsh sailors readily faced the challenge of unchartered voyages of adventure. Welsh seamen were numbered among the Elizabethan sea dogs.

Welsh trading vessels increased in number with the commercial prosperity of the Tudors. Protective Navigation Laws ensured the carrying of goods in British vessels.

In the seventeenth century the natural wealth of the Principality was developed. Minerals and ores were exported from the small Welsh ports. The import trade was increased to meet the needs of a growing population. Smuggling prospered. Coastal trade was carried on long after the steamship had signalled the end of the old sailing ships.

Direct knowledge of the early ships is scanty, but there is evidence that corporations granted burghers' rights to shipwrights and carpenters. There were shipyards at Cardigan, Milford Haven, Carmarthen, Aberaeron, Aberystwyth, Barmouth and Caernarvon.

It was usual for a ship to be built on a fine stretch of sandy soil at the head of a tidal creek. The ship could be launched easily because of its proximity to the sea.

Timber for shipbuilding was specially grown. Oak was suitable for shipbuilding. Many a landed squire invested heavily in forests of oak. The trees were trimmed so as to provide natural crooks and knee timbers. Larch trees were valued in that they provided 'knees' for small boats, serving to hold the thwarts to the timber. Pine poles were used for masts. Elm was used for the keel. Timber was sent to the shipwright's yard in its green state. It seasoned naturally during the long process of building a boat.

The time spent in building depended on the size of the boat. Two years of regular work was an average. The bark, *Ordovic* (825 tons), built in Port Dinorwic in 1877, took more than three years to build.

The timber was sawn in the shipyard into plankings. These planks were assembled according to size and use and were stacked, much in the manner of corn stocks, the air circulating between them.

Mapped out in chalk on the floor of the shipwright's loft was a plan of the vessel to be built. The design was drawn in full size for smaller craft. A wooden template was made of the various parts. These could be carried into the shipyard. The timbers, both heavy and light, could be hewn and sawn into pattern.

A large heavy adze was a foremost tool in the shipyard. When they had been cut to size and shape, the heavy timbers were taken to the slipway and assembled on keel blocks.

A single trunk was used for smaller vessels. Two or more trunks were needed for larger ships. Stem and stern posts were of oak. The stern post called for fine timber, massive and straight. The long wooden pins, known as treenails or trunnels, used in fastening the planks of the ship to the timbers, were also of oak. They were superior to iron bolts which would have corroded.

Oaken crooks with a natural curve formed the hull. The timbers were adze-hewn on the flat to the required measurements, and were then raised into position with the aid of a derrick. The inner timbers were laid over the keel and bound; the floor timbers were of elm. Cross shelves spanned the ribs supporting the decks. These gave additional strength to the hull. The shelves were secured by 'knees' formed of natural forks of timber.

When the framework of the ship was complete, ship's carpenters began the work of sheathing the framework, both within and without. Crevices between planks were filled with oakum which had been soaked in pitch or tar, to make it watertight.

Masts called forth the skill of an army of craftsmen – sailmakers,

1 *Titus Hoad of Farmers, Dyfed (aged ten) demonstrates his flair for spinning*

2 ABOVE *E. Hetherington shows how to make a fringe on a travelling rug at the British Legion woollen factory, Llanwrtyd Wells.* 3 BELOW *Smock in Welsh wool from Snowdon Mill, Portmadoc*

4 ABOVE *Embroidery: crewel work in wool on Welsh flannel.*

5 BELOW *Quilting: bed quilt and cushion*

6 ABOVE *An old-time dry-stone waller on the Welsh Border.*

7 BELOW *Eighteenth-century slate memorial slabs at Llangaddock Gwent*

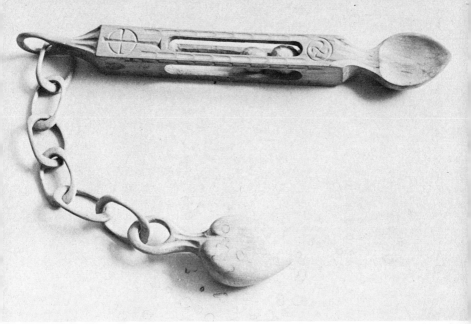

8 ABOVE *A lovespoon of hardened oak made in the traditional way from a single piece of wood.* 9 BELOW *Wood carving of a golden eagle by Handel Edwards of Skewen, Swansea*

10 Wood turner at work: Gwyndaf Breese at the Folk Museum, St Fagan's

11 ABOVE *Clog making: Hywel Davies of Tregaron using a clogger's knife.* 12 BELOW *A clogger in the woods near Abergavenny: from an old photograph*

13 *Leather worker, Fishguard, with some of his work*

14 *An old photograph of spelk basket-makers (Y Cymro)*

15 ABOVE *Making corn dollies.* 16 BELOW *Refectory table in Welsh oak and rush seated-chairs, by Philip Wilson of Harlech*

17 ABOVE *Wrought-ironwork forecourt gates at Chirk Castle,
Denbighshire by the Davies Brothers.* 18 BELOW *Roger Thomas,
blacksmith of Llanelli with a prize-winning candelabra made by him*

19 ABOVE *Wood-fired hand-thrown pottery by Dafydd Jones.*

20 BELOW *Pottery: a selection of products from the Taurus Pottery, Anglesey*

21 ABOVE *Nantgarw porcelain: plate painted at the factory by Thomas Pardoe.* 22 BELOW *A hand-painted Nantgarw teapot and stand*

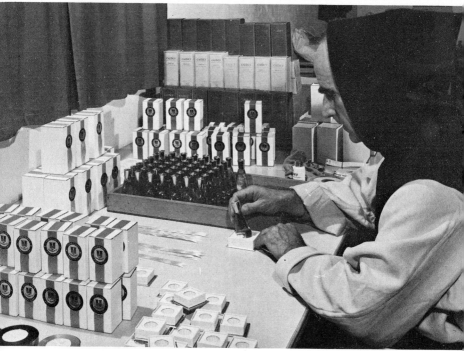

23 ABOVE *John Thomas of Gwaelod-y-Garth making a harp.*

24 BELOW *A monk at Caldey Abbey packing perfume*

25 *Marjory Carter making Bedfordshire lace on a bolster or 'dumpy' using bobbins*

26 RIGHT *Glass blowing: an ornament by Vincenzo Speranza of Saundersfoot.* 27 BELOW *Polished stone jewellery*

ropemakers and smiths. A carved figurehead in wood was placed on the prow.

The launching of the ship was the occasion of a public holiday. If the boat had been built on ground slightly inland, willing hands came to cut a waterway to the sea. When the ship was on the water the master-builder gave a dinner to his friends and fellow-workmen. Then the ship was rigged with masts and sails and ropes. A big ship would have square sails that would take it across the ocean. One-masted sloops and smacks were more usual in the small coastal shipyards of Wales.

The canal mania which affected Britain in the eighteenth and nineteenth centuries also affected Wales, although here it was tempered by the hilly nature of the country. Yet a network of canals was made, linking inland industrial centres with the sea. Wooden flat-bottomed boats were built for use on those canals.

The building of ships provided much work. David Thomas (*Hen Longau a Llongwyr Cymru*) records that 60 ships were built in ten years at Barmouth in the decade 1779–88. 150 ships were built in 20 years 1788–1807 at Pwllheli. During the nineteenth century more than a thousand ships were built at Caernarvon. From 200 to 300 ships were built during the first half of the same century at Aberystwyth, Aberaeron, New Quay and Cardigan.

The home-built vessels had a democratic ownership. The boats were not owned by a limited comany, but were the property of the men who manned and loaded them. Often they were partly owned by the craftsmen who had built them, by the shop-keepers of the harbour town, and by the farmers who watched the boat open her sails to the welcoming wind, as they followed the plough on the headland.

By legal stipulation, a boat was calculated in 64 shares. Four shares formed an ounce, and these were auctioned publicly. There was risk in investing in a share, but there was also the prospect of lucrative dividends.

WALKING STICKS

Fashions in accessories, like fashion in dress, travel in cycles. Walking sticks, though less in evidence at the present time, add to the pleasures of a walker; they are the treasured and invaluable companions of the elderly and the handicapped. There are connoisseurs who collect walking sticks, seeking with a practised eye for traditional woods such as oak, ash and cherry, among the many inferior timbers that flood the market.

In rural areas the making of walking sticks is a craft that still exists, although it has become rarer. The interest of agricultural organisations and shows, and also of eisteddfodau, has helped considerably to keep it alive. Competitions are held for the best-made walking stick.

Here the work of the craftsman begins with the handling of *living* material. It is also controlled by seasonal conditions. By choice, the stick is cut in November or December, or possibly January. At this time the sap in the plant is at its lowest. If it is cut at any other time, the bark will shrink. When the wood is set out to dry, it will be subject to cracking.

The craftsman is prepared to spend considerable time in searching for the right timber. A prolonged search, which may have its beginnings several seasons before, may result in the finding of only a few good and suitable pieces. Some areas are more productive in their yield than others. A locality may become well-known among those searching for material. As a result, a copse or wood soon becomes denuded. Then the makers of walking sticks move away to other places, taking with them their tools and accessories – saws, and small hatchets and sacking, to protect the bark of the wood when it is cut.

Much wood has to be eliminated as the walking-stick maker seeks meticulously for a straight length of material. He makes a close search where the trees grow in close proximity. Here, branching out is at a minimum, for the side twigs grow upwards towards the light. Such growth is important in ash and in hazel; knots on the stick detract from its appearance. Knots tend to be prevalent in ash. The craftsman knows that the ash with the fewest blemishes, grows in sheltered places. When searching in a hazel copse, the craftsman may find excellent specimens as they appear above ground. Beneath the soil, however, the roots grow in a tangled mass. He cuts into this to obtain wood to form a handle. Many potential sticks are abandoned, as, when the handle is being shaped, deep cracks and black lines appear indicating the roots of branches. A vigilant watch is kept for these flaws. Seldom does the craftsman work on wood that has not been allowed to rest for at least a year.

On occasions, the craftsman will trim the tip of a young sapling, producing growth that is acceptable. If he uses this method he can apply his own particular technique and introduce his own idiosyncracies and decoration. Spiral cuts along the stick can result in the formation of outgrowths that form a pattern. A drawback of the treatment of a living stick is that, as the result of incision, the sapling tends to deteriorate; further, it ceases to grow upward. Hence it may fall below the standard length of a walking stick, and despite expert care over many weeks it will die.

Infinite patience is essential in the maker of walking sticks. Following a careful search for suitable wood, he must make sure that it is fully seasoned before he starts work on it. He stores the wood, wrapping it in sacking to make sure that the process of dying is slowed down. The part of the stick which is to form the handle is buried in moist earth for the same purpose. It also safeguards against the possibility of cracks forming. After a period of approximately a year the craftsman examines the wood, speculating on making a handle.

When makers of walking sticks compete against each other, special regard is given to the measurements and also the shape of a walking stick. There is a measure of discrimination. A man's stick has a standard length of three feet and one inch. A woman's stick is shorter and allows for personal taste.

The weight and balance of the stick are important. A stick of constant thickness tends to be heavy and cumbersome. Consequently, it is tapered. This varies in range, but a usual reckoning is from one inch in diameter at the handle, to half an inch at the tip of the stick. Weight is thus reduced, and firmness at the base is increased. There is another essential – balance. This must be true, else the other features are almost worthless. The accepted point of balance is at a spot one third of the length measured from the handle. The handle must be at a right angle from the stem. This ensures that the walker's weight falls directly over the tip of the stick.

Individuality characterises the handle of a stick. It may vary widely in shape, and also in material. Most curve slightly on the upper side, so that a comfortable hold on the palm of the hand is ensured. Some craftsmen stress individuality, making no two handles alike on the grounds that no two persons have hands that are alike. Others are less specialised; they have a set pattern of handles, but allow for slight variations.

Before the handle is shaped or fixed, the stem is examined for any bends. Prevailing winds cause these, but they can be eliminated by careful drying. The stick is laid to rest. A bend is sometimes oiled and heated near an open fire. Treatment varies according to the wood. Response varies widely too. Hazelwood reacts slowly, whereas a blackthorn is more pliable and the process of straightening is less difficult.

The craftsman often works on several sticks at the same time. When forming handles, he makes a number of rough shapings and then, using a penknife, he introduces finer work. He deliberately eschews the modern tools which are used in woodcraft today. The details of carving an animal or bird are created with the help of small carving tools. A scraper, or glass paper is used, to introduce smoothness to the handle. An old craftsman will achieve the result with a piece of broken glass. When the desired smoothness has been achieved, a permanent polish is introduced. A usual process is to apply shellac in several layers. After each application the handle is rubbed with glass paper. By such methods, the polish becomes translucent, smooth and permanent.

When stem and handle are not formed from one entire piece, the stick is created from two pieces. Such a stick, wherein the handle is affixed, is regarded as inferior in craftsmanship, weaker in strength, and less comfortable in use. Such sticks, however, are very serviceable, and the dearth of suitable material necessitates their use.

The craftsman has but few tools. He has a boiler, a press, and a fixed knife. Sometimes he uses a circulating cutting saw and a lathe. Polishing buffs help him to bring the highlights of the material to the surface.

Measurement is important when making the handle. Its diameter at the wider end is approximately three quarters of an inch. This corresponds to the stem of the stick. The stem is fitted into the horn, and fixed with a strong adhesive.

In fashioning a shepherd's crook, the craftsman draws on the same techniques. His search for material to create a crook is more arduous. The standard length is five feet and six inches. Pride of place lies in the crook. This varies in shape and size with locality. Functionalism, however, demands that the curve should be sufficient to hook a sheep by the neck, and that a smaller curve, which is part of the whole, should be of a size and shape to hook a recalcitrant sheep by the leg without injuring it. Strength and delicacy are essential features of the crook itself.

A thumb stick is another example of the craft. It is often made of cherrywood or blackthorn. There is a natural fork at the top. There is less stringency about the length of this stick. It ranges between three feet eight inches and four feet six inches. There are variations in the forks, known as plain, handle or knobby.

TOYS

The firm of *R. I. and S. Hughes of Harlech, Gwynedd*, specialises in quality toys that are completely individual in design and finish. A variety of things for the home is also made, such as lamps, bowls, bread boards, stools, benches, settles and coffee tables.

Toys are designed with originality, and with due regard to their psychological and educational value. Safety first precautions have led to the use of lead-free oil primers made specially for the purpose.

The firm has produced a rocking horse design based on one that was much in use in the early seventeenth century. High-backed seating has been arranged for the safety of the young rider. The body and head are made of oak, and the rockers are of plywood. Wool is used for the mane, and the reins are made out of plaited twine.

A speciality is a jousting horse. The child stands in a box with two straps across his shoulders. There is a material surround to the horse, hence the mediaeval name, jousting horse. There is also a hobby horse with a plywood head painted grey with black and white spots.

Rocking cribs, pull-along bricks, rattles, jig-saws, lorries, trucks, go-carts, prams, toy soldiers, trains, tractors, oak Noah's Arks, and farm buildings, are also made.

Acorn Workshops, at Milton, near Pembroke, Dyfed, directed by Roger Jones, a former social worker, produce unusual musical instruments. A 24-stringed psaltery modelled on a design popular in the Middle Ages is produced there. An African thumb-piano and a miniature version of a Welsh harp, are also produced.

At first Mr. Jones specialised in making toys, and then widened his activities to making money boxes, milking stools and sailing boats. Emphasis is placed on the creation of products which are characterised by a special quality of their own. Mr. Roger Jones has strong views about craftsmanship. He stands firm against an industrial set-up. Faced with imperative expansion, Mr. Jones is firm in his decision that the business shall not turn into a production line set-up. He said: 'I would then become a businessman and not a craftsman. I prefer to be in the sawdust of the workshop, and not in the office chair.'

The accent is invariably on natural finished woods, of which many varieties are used. Traditional toys and original models are made with an emphasis on durability – boats, vehicles, trains and carts; also, dolls and dolls' cradles; Noah's Arks with hand-sculptured animals, lay-out sets, Nativity sets, dolls' houses. Of special interest are individually-designed rocking horses made from hardwoods, in Georgian and Victorian styles. They are made in natural honey-toned pine, or have a traditional dapple finish with real hair, and with leather accoutrements.

Welsh Children's Games and Pastimes by Canon D. Parry Jones*, gives an authoritative and comprehensive account of the subject, in particular of the playthings of a country child in Wales in the early decades of the century. He writes:

> 'There were very few dolls and bought toys in those days; still, the children were not left destitute of playthings, for fathers, elder brothers and especially farm servants were adept at making little things for their amusement. For example, they made "raddles" (rattles), plaiting them in straw or rushes, into which two marbles, shells, or small stones were put, and behold a rattle that could not fail to satisfy any infant eager for noise.'

He gives illuminating accounts of such playthings as the pop gun, the bow and arrow, the whistle and mouth organ, and tops and kites, most of them being made at home.

> 'Hoops were one of the few things we did not make ourselves, but all the same, we saw them made. When their season arrived, we would receive father's permission to call on Sam, the blacksmith, to ask him to make us one. We had not only the thrill of ordering a hoop, but the pleasure of watching it in the making. Our eyes followed Sam, as he selected one of the long slender iron rods from a stock that he had got in readiness. Having measured it, and cut off the right length, he began hammering it on one of the angles of the anvil, and as he did so, we could see

*Gee and Son, Denbigh, 1964.

the curve growing, until in the end, the two ends met in a circle. They were then put in the fire until they were red-hot, and finally, hammered together into one round piece, and lo! our hoop was made. But there was one thing yet to come, and that was to put it in a tub of cold water, where it sizzled and threw up a cloud of steam. It was left there while he fashioned the hook or bowly. Then, taking the hoop out of the tub, giving it here and there a few taps on the anvil, he threw it into motion towards the door – in this manner did we always receive our hoops. Off we went after it and out through the door, happy as boys have always been from the days of Ancient Greece, following a hoop.'

Toys became incorporated into the educational system. An interesting application in Wales has come about with the rise of bi-lingual education. Toys are in general use now, to teach the Welsh language and also to practise it.

～5～
Leatherwork

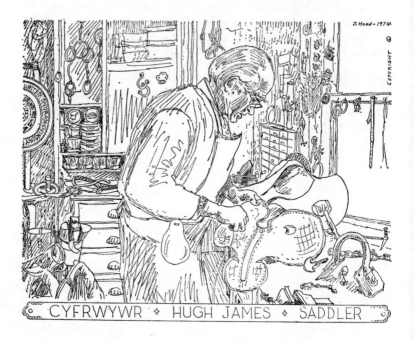

CYFRWYWR ❖ HUGH JAMES ❖ SADDLER

Amongst particular craftsmen in leather may be mentioned:

Bryncroes, Aberdaron Gwynedd. On the west side of Mynydd Rhiw, Melinda Holt of Tyddyn makes high fashion accessories in leather in beautiful soft cowhide. The work is tooled and embossed. Unusual buckles are a speciality.

Candles in the Rain, Nant Glyn, Denbigh, Clwyd. Handbags and shoulder bags are made in top grain bridle leather. The leather goods made include saddle stools, jewellery boxes, belts and watchstraps.

Pinnochio, Carmarthen Road, Saundersfoot, Dyfed. David Thomas Palmer uses highest quality British hides which are prepared, tooled and dyed on the premises.

Fron Fawr, Boncath, Dyfed. Ray Cori has revived the ancient craft of making bottles, jugs, tankards and mugs in leather.

The firm of J. W. Wycherley & Son at Malpas on the Welsh border has specialised in leather work since 1859. There is a head saddler assisted by five craftsmen.

The making of saddles is a speciality. The saddles are produced in the Malpas workshop. They range from the felt pad which is the cheapest form of saddle, to the spring all-purpose saddle, which is covered in hide. Other varieties are the general purpose saddle, the sloping head jumping saddle, the hunting saddle, the racing saddle, and the show saddle.

Saddle trees are supplied to the firm by tree makers. Curriers supply the leather. The head saddler designs the style of saddle. On an average calculation, a spring saddle is one man's work for a week. To speed up cutting and making, it is more usual to start a batch of ten trees, and perform the cutting and sewing on a conveyor system. Detailed attention is given to special orders requiring saddles to fit individual horses. Leather accessories such as spectacle cases, and leather folders and wallets, are made. The firm produces all its own bridle work. This is cut and made in batches of ten articles.

The saddler has always had plenty of work. Today, when saddlers are fewer, the proportion of work has increased relatively. The saddler now supplies saddles and riding equipment, hand-made show and in-hand bridles, and a wide range of traditional leather goods mainly in cow-hide. He makes and supplies high-class travel goods, and hand-made belts. Further, he is much in demand as a repairer and as a contriver.

Some leather-workers have a department specialising in sheep-skins, lambskins and suede. Clothing in these media are made and sold – coats, hats, gloves, leggings, boots, shoes, slippers, and also travel and floor rugs. Special commissions are undertaken for the making of tankards, buckets and umbrella stands.

In the heart of Radnorshire, at *Beguildy*, Ray Nicklin and Pam Evans have their leather workshop. Theirs is a small firm. Their products are their own recommendation. They have no time for the usual commercial enterprises such as advertising and competitive salesmanship, for they are engaged full time in producing their products to meet a big and steady demand.

Sycamore Leather prides itself on doing everything by hand – cutting, tooling, staining, thonging, finishing and polishing. They even make their own embossing tools and their own polishes. Bees-wax is used to give a fine polish. The leather is tanned by hand. It is, in consequence, oily and supple, and it has the advantage of having the natural topgrain left on it.

A wide range of leather goods are made from best quality British hide. Sycamore Leather make travelling bags, shoulder bags, belts and smaller items, and individual special commissions.

SHOEMAKERS AND COBBLERS

When the leather industries were centred in rural Wales a boot-maker was a usual figure in the villages. He made shoes from leather bought locally, and the cobbler repaired them. The shoemaker measured his client's foot, then making a wooden last as a model. He was meticulous in choosing the right kind of leather. Care and accuracy went into the making of the boot or shoe, so as to ensure ease in comfort and wear.

When factories provided light smart shoes, often of greater comfort, the country shoemaker became, overnight, a cobbler. It was useless for the shoemaker to compete with the cheaper mass-produced goods.

The bootmaker had, as his last stronghold, the hillside villages where there was a demand for heavy boots. When the small tanneries moved to the urban centres his supply of local material failed and he joined the ranks of shoe repairers. Nowadays, a very few craftsmen among the shoe repairers of Wales can make boots and shoes, as well as being capable of repairing them. In the mountaineering districts of Wales there may yet arise, as in Scotland and the Lake District, centres where shoemakers will build boots and shoes of quality, to serve individual needs and tastes. The leather craftsmen of Wales can maintain their good reputation with its high standard of workmanship and personal integrity.

HORN

A horn cup was a prominent article of ceremonial use in the old Celtic feasts. The early drinking horn was kept much in its natural form. The rim was sometimes given a metal band, mainly as a means of strengthening, but also as a form of decoration. The earlier drinking vessels had no stands. Their use was communal, and the absence of a stand resulted in their being passed continuously from one drinker to another. Individual drinking vessels had no stands either; they were in reality *tumblers*. When three- or four-footed stands were provided for the drinking horns they were often ornate.

In mediaeval times horn was valued highly as a material. Its use was not confined to drinking vessels; it was used for cups, spoons, handles, and for such purposes as powder boxes and flasks. The peculiar qualities of horn, its imperviousness to damp and to acid, remain; its fall into disuse is hard to understand.

In laboratory and in kitchen, the horn spoon continues in use. Whereas colours and tastes cling to spoons of wood and of metal, horn spoons do not take on the flavour of a substance, no matter how long they have been immersed in it. Horn spoons are light and remain smooth and clean-surfaced, showing no signs of splitting or of bending. They are graded according to capacity for weight, and thus form an easy form of measurement. They are superior to metal spoons, in that they do not burn the lips when sipping from them.

The horn spoon for table use is now seldom seen, but it must have been an object of beauty on older tables gleaming under sub-dued lights. Miss Dorothy Hartley has written:

'Once I saw a black oak table polished with beeswax. On it stood twelve slender black horn tumbers. They fluted upwards from ebony to creamy white. There were black and white horn-handled knives to match, simple, practical, modern, yet old as the hills.'

Some day the beauty as well as the utility of horn for the table will be recognised again.

Some of the old horn spoons had silver mountings, but those in general use were plain. It was considered a great asset to possess spoons which were carefully matched. Different breeds of cattle provided spoons of various sizes and lengths, for example long-horned cattle provided long-handled spoons.

The supply of horn was dependent on the routes used by the drovers. These 'economic ships of state' were powerful factors in the economic and social life of Wales from the fourteenth century onward. In his book *Y Ffordd yng Nghymru* Professor R. T. Jenkins explains the direction of the traditional drover routes of Wales. The drover was intent on conveying his herd of a thousand beasts or more by a route that would ensure an average safety for man and beast. He sought a way where water and fodder were easily obtained. The drover routes over the Welsh hills converge on the Welsh Border, centring in the south on Gloucester and on Bristol, linking up the Marches of Wales, and also forming a way for Irish cattle, journeying from Holyhead to Liverpool.

On the outskirts of the larger and more easterly market towns were tanneries and soap factories and horn works.

In these, horns were classified into those of oxen and sheep. Deer horn was sometimes preserved here, its use being valued for knife and other handles. Young horns are smooth and yield readily to polishing. Older horns show ridges which sometimes prove intractable, and which detract from the finish of polished work.

The horn worker would sort out the horns according to the breed of the cattle. The horn of Welsh cattle was specially treasured because of its susceptibility to a high natural polish, and the beauty of its black and white marking. The cattle of Shropshire and of Herefordshire provided horn renowned for strength and wearing qualities.

The horn worker removed the 'flint' or hard filling from inside the horn. At one time this horny substance was used for soap making. It was taken to the soap factory adjacent to the horn works. Where possible the horn maker liked to cut objects from the horn in its natural state, but for flat objects he was obliged to heat the horn. He removed the tip. Then the horn was split down one side. Next it was subjected to steaming and heating in an oven. After this it was flattened in a press. Horn is particularly amenable to such processes and responds in a most obliging way. The horn worker used but few tools. Besides his boiler and press, he had a special tool in the form of a fixed knife. Certain objects demand the use of a circulating cutting saw and a lathe. Polishing buffs enabled him to bring the highlights of his material to the surface.

HORSE-HAIR HALTERS

The making of horse-hair halters was, until the coming of the motor-car, a widespread craft. Knowledge of the technique employed survives, and there are still a few who practise the craft.

The halters are particularly strong, and are attractive items on horses in full dress. The raw material is now somewhat scarce.

White horse-hair is used in the main. First, it is prepared for spinning. It is placed in a pan and shaken free of all tangles. The collection of hair is rolled up and folded over to form a loop. A smaller supply of black horse-hair is prepared in the same way.

The next stage is spinning. The end of the first strand of hair is attached to a wooden spinner or 'thod'. Two people are involved in the spinning. Dexterity is needed in the process. A thread is taken from the bundle. The spinner deftly twists it into a thicker thread, and ensures an evenness in the twist. The second spinner rolls a length of the prepared thread on to the wooden thod.

The spinner aims at spinning about five yards at a time. The required length is about 18 yards.

The halter-maker and his assistant then prepare a smaller amount of black horse-hair. A longer piece of black hair is woven to make it easier to join the two threads for weaving. The black strands are inserted into the white for the purpose of weaving and plaiting.

The next stage is carried on out of doors. A hook is driven into a tree trunk or a post. The white thread is attached to this. A yard-stick (*prenllathen*) is used to measure the length. Measuring from the end attached to the hook, a third of the total length is marked. This third section is plaited with the black to form a two-ply strand. This is then rolled on to a wooden hook (*bachyn*). This implement resembles a forked stick. By a process called four-to-one, this hook is again used. In the final plaiting, the six-in-one process is done by hand. Three strands of two-ply horse-hair are used.

The halter is then examined and tested for strength, after being fastened around a tree.

The woven material, attractive and strong, is next shaped into a halter and head-piece for a pony or horse.

TANNERIES

Tanning ranked with the manufacture of cloth as the chief staple industry of mediaeval Wales. Along the roads the drovers trod there were established, at intervals, tanneries, where good use was made of the ready supply of native oak bark for the tanning of leather. By Tudor days, tanners had organised themselves into guilds.

The tanner was an important personality in the community. He provided materials for the bootmaker, the saddler, the glover, and for numerous other craftsmen who required leather in some process of their work. The tanner was a man of social and financial standing. He could expect no quick return for his labour, and he had to have sufficient financial security to tie up part at least of his capital for at least two years, while a supply of hides was being tanned. His reputation was usually high; his leathers were worth purchasing.

The superiority of country-tanned leathers over their factory counterparts is acknowledged to this day.

The tanneries of Wales were fortunate in the proximity of a plentiful supply of running water in the rivers. Water which is soft and free from iron deposits is of special worth for tanning purposes.

Changes in agriculture have affected the tanner. In the days before farmers had learnt to grow winter feeding crops, flocks and herds were killed in the autumn. The farmer received plentiful supplies of fells and hides. With improvement in stock-rearing, cattle were killed when they were younger. The hides were, therefore, not so tough; the leather was not so strong.

Tanneries, which specialised in cattle hides, produced strong leather for harness, boots and strops. When slaughter houses were set up in the busy industrial centres of Wales, the country tannery lost its ready supply of hides. For a period some of the Welsh tanneries, faced with the competition of the larger English tanneries, managed to maintain part of their identity by becoming appendages of the bigger establishments. They often served as receiving houses for the fells and hides.

The bark of Welsh oak was considered especially suitable for tanning. It was cut in the spring when the sap was rising. It has been superseded today by imported concentrated extracts of bark and acorns.

In the traditional processes, oak bark was crushed in the tannery and then soaked in a pit of water. The strong solution obtained was then transferred into a series of pits. Just as the wool sorter will classify the various wools on a sheep, so will a tanner sort out the particular sections of the hides. The backs of the hides are reserved for sole leather, the sides are used for uppers and saddles; belly leather, being lighter, was kept for lighter articles.

In order to loosen the hair on the hides by dissolving the cells of the epidermis, the skins are immersed and rotated for a period of about three weeks in a bath of milk of caustic lime. In this way, the pores of the skin fill up; the greater this action, the softer and looser the resultant leather. The loosened hair is removed by scraping on a sloping round wooden beam by means of a two-handled knife.

Leather meant for soles is washed with water and the lime removed. Hides intended for softer leather are treated more carefully and reduced from their swollen condition to one of flaccidity and softness. Fermenting infusions of excrement are used to hasten this process; that of pigeons and fowls is used for hides and skins, and that of dogs for finer leathers.

Next, the hides are prepared for tanning with vegetable materials, for 'tawing' with alum and salt, or with chrome tannages.

The hides are immersed in the solution. They are moved frequently after ten days or so, then they are placed in stronger solutions. After several weeks of treatment, they are frequently sprinkled. In the later stages, a dry 'dusting' material such as ground bark is applied.

Sole leather is finished by stretching and smoothing and rolling. The leather must be partially dried before it is rolled. Leathers used for the uppers of heavy boots are limed. Then they are coloured in weak and old tanning liquors. Currying follows on all the heavier leathers intended for harness and belting, and where flexibility is required. The leather is impregnated with fats and oils; it is also scoured, stretched, shaved and smoothed. Goatskins were used for making morocco leather. The skin of young lambs was made into glove kid. Boots were made from calf kid.

The small North Wales tanneries, at one period, specialised in producing roller leather for covering steel rollers in the Lancashire cotton mills. The Welsh mountain-bred sheep yielded skins particularly suitable for this purpose. The sheep had been subjected to hard weather, and consequently the skin was close-grained and strong.

The local supply of sheepskins was plentiful, and as a subsidiary craft the tanneries supplied wool for lining gloves. Warm floor rugs were made from sheepskins. These were sometimes dyed in delicate pastel shades; more frequently they were left in their natural state.

6

Grass

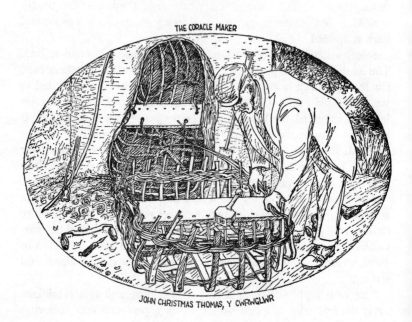

THE CORACLE MAKER

JOHN CHRISTMAS THOMAS, Y CWRWGLWR

THATCHING

The Anglo-Saxon word *thaec* – thatch, meant simply a roof. With time it came to mean a covering of straw or of rushes placed on the roofs of buildings, or on stacks of hay or of grain.

The use of vegetable matter as a roof covering is very old. Clods of earth were in all probability placed on the wattle huts of early tribes. These coverings developed into things of greater usefulness and of beauty. Thatch of a primitive kind was used not only for vernacular buildings, but also sometimes for ecclesiastical structures in a temporary or semi-permanent capacity. The timber and earth construction of the motte and bailey castle was probably covered with thatch, as doubtless were the dwelling quarters of Norman times. The bareness of some buildings, as they appear today, is often explained by the fact that a warm, thick, over-lapping covering of thatch has been removed from a sparser covering of slates or tiles. It is likely that some mediaeval buildings, meant to be roofed, only received a covering of thatch which was intended to be temporary, pending completion of the whole.

In the upland areas of Wales, where supplies of straw are limited, any suitable vegetable matter to hand was used, just as it is today for ricks. In the rich corn-growing valleys, plentiful supplies of straw were available. In the fertile Vale of Glamorgan and in the timber and plaster areas of the Severn Valley, farmhouses and cottages in compact villages preserve a tradition of skilled thatching different from, and in some ways superior to, the thatched roofs and ricks of the Welsh crofts.

It was in a natural evolution that settled man covered his roof-tree, first with grass and then with heather, rush or stalks of corn, packing the material closely together, after the manner of birds with their nests. The nine-roomed palace traditional to an early Welsh king would thus be roofed.

Thatch was common in the Middle Ages, and continued as a popular covering long after man had explored the possibilities of fissile stone. A thatched roof was cheaper. It required a lighter roof-tree. According to what was native to the district, man used reeds, rushes, sedge, fern, furze, bracken – materials easily available with only the cost of labour. When men learnt to sow grass and to harvest it, they realised how appropriate corn stalks were as a covering for roofs. Then, growing dextrous in the use of it, they fashioned it into coverings of beauty. A tradition of thatch gradually became established in certain localities. Men clung to the comfort of the familiar, and unconsciously recognised the affinity between a material and the surrounding landscape.

Local styles of thatching inevitably developed. Some were simple; some were elaborate, catering for gables and roof ornamentation. The art of the thatcher is distinctly an individual one. The work of a particular thatcher can be detected. Individual styles are traditional for, like many other country crafts, thatching is often hereditary in families.

Thatching was used not only on the cob cottages and crofts, but

W.C.—G

also as a covering for outhouses and hayricks found in the valleys or open moorlands. Such thatching was often crude, that in the stackyard being more so than that on the house, for its duration was brief.

People living in Wales know that the onslaught of south-westerly gales demands a sound roof. An under-thatch of heather, fern or some similar material was sometimes placed beneath the thatch proper. The under-thatch was secured to the roof timbers with straw. These double layers were usual on crofts in the hills of Snowdonia and Plynlimmon.

A fine tradition of thatching was evolved in the Vale of Glamorgan, with its generous supplies of straw. In the area there are many excellent examples of local style.

The low-pitched roofs so evident in the Principality are the outcome of climate and of position. They are built in this manner so that the gales blow over them in an upward sweep, instead of buffeting against a two-storey wall. The roof timbers on which thatchers lay the thatch are usually of very simple design. Ancient builders were often content to use rough wood, often with the bark intact, for rafters and laths. They employed timber found close at hand, and made no effort to hew out irregularities. Sometimes timbers from old ships were used. Many a curving covering of thatch in the Vale of Glamorgan may well rest on beams that have sailed the seven seas. Roofs were sometimes constructed so that they projected over the house walls, providing wide eaves. The thatchers emphasised these eaves, carrying the lowest layer of straw well out over the walls. This was a distinct advantage in cob cottages, and in buildings where the walls were porous, for the water was carried away directly from the roof. The strip of ground on which the drippings from the eaves fell was waste. An eaves-dropper was one who came creeping beneath the overhanging edge of the roof to listen, illicitly, to what was being said within the house.

The hand-reaping of the straw of the Vale of Glamorgan is believed to account largely for the excellence and durability of the thatching. In the days when the reaping was done with a sickle, the stubble was left to stand in the sun. The cropping of the corn close to the ear rendered the stubble long enough for thatching. When corn was threshed by hand care was taken that the tubular stems were not crushed or flattened. The thatchers had in this way material that was compact and waterproof.

The thatched roofs of the houses in the Vale of Glamorgan show wide sweeps of flowing curves. Some have a generous thickening in the middle section of the pitch. This is a protection against runnels of rain which tend to wear a hollow in the thatch. A bulge or convex curve results in the pitch of the roof falling more steeply to the eaves. When a steeper pitch is required a 'backbone' of straw is laid on the rafters or under-thatch. The steeper the pitch the more easily the rain falls off at a good angle. Undulating thatch is achieved by covering roof timbers that have a hipped formation. The thatchers are skilled in making the cosy covering assume odd shapes, clustering around chimneys and gables. The thatcher sometimes tiles dormer windows, and uses slates to form gutters in the depression between them.

In the more western areas of Wales thatching is, by tradition, of a cruder kind. It was secured by ropes made of straw or rush and weighted with stones. Such work was often done by an amateur: the farmer and his labourer in the more leisurely periods of the year.

Apart from its picturesque appearance, the great advantage of thatch is one that has always been recognised – its liability to modify extremes of heat and cold. Moreover, as thatch is light, the roof timbers could be correspondingly of light structure.

One of the main disadvantages of thatch is its ability to fire. To counteract this, chimneys were made disproportionately high.

BASKET-MAKING

Basket-making was a craft practised by primitive tribes in Britain, for example by people of the Iron Age, as in the Glastonbury Lake Village. The lightness and pliancy of the willow was pleasing to the early inhabitants of Wales, who used it prodigally, not only for their utensils but for their homes, their boats and their equipment in war. The technique of basket-making has changed little through the centuries, and the craft has in the main resisted the use of the machine.

The style of basketry has changed inevitably with the passage of time. The tendency has been for the craft to become urbanised. Yet the solitary basket-maker still exists and produces work of a high standard. Charitable organisations, such as institutes for the blind, have concentrated on basket-work, and have produced excellent work. The willow rods are capable of easy transport, and men in towns – often disabled men – work co-operatively, making finely finished goods. Basket-making of today tends to be more specialised in its output, and the one-time craftsman of the rural area who could produce strong skeps as well as delicate work baskets is fast becoming a rarity.

Willow rods were grown haphazardly in Wales, but in conjunction with other efforts to develop the craft of basket-making, attempts have been made from time to time to systematise the growing of osiers. Forestry organisations have schemes for the cultivation of osiers in Dyfed. Schemes did not always prove successful, but valuable knowledge resulted from the experiments.

The technique employed in the making of willow baskets is ancient. It gave rise to the craft of textile weaving, and contributed to the development of the art of the potter. Before the potter's wheel was in use, vessels of clay were shaped in moulds made of basketry. The imprint of the woven rods on the clay formed the earliest designs on pottery. Early Britons used huts and boats of wattle. The manipulation of the rods to form baskets remains unchanged from early days of civilisation.

Furniture, both for indoor and outdoor use, was made in basketry, and also babies' cradles. Manuscripts dating from the twelfth century testify to this. The willow rods plaited together form light, durable articles, which are easily cleaned.

Structural development and changing fashions have resulted in the abandoning of many basket-work articles which were much in use in the past. Castle and cottage of mediaeval times were structures of wattle covered with daub. Carriages had baskets with hoods. Creels were usual on the seashore, and basket panniers were strapped to the donkeys that travelled through Wales.

SPELK BASKETS

Farm work demands strong baskets. Trugs are made from split oak or ash, with the frames of willow or of birch. They are in a variety of shapes, and in the main serve local needs. Farm hands, priding themselves on their versatility, made baskets of the left-hand and of the right-hand type. These were fitted with a strap, not a handle, and were made to rest on right hip or left. Kidney-shaped trugs or skips or slops were made for carrying in front. Such baskets were strongly made, and could be used for carrying fodder or stones.

Spelk baskets are made from rent oak; swills or slops or skips are made of cleft willow twigs. Such baskets are often oval shaped. They vary in size, but they are usually two or three feet wide. Their strong qualities and open shape make them useful for carrying corn, potatoes and coal; they are used on the coast to carry fish.

The housewife used them as clothes baskets, and they were used as cradles when softly lined. A mesh work of cleft willow twigs was an ideal riddle or sieve for use in a corn mill. Craftsmen were employed by millers to provide such equipment.

The maker of spelk baskets was careful in the selection of his material. He cut oak from a nearby coppice, and then stacked it in the open and near his home. He cut poles from four to six feet in length and removed the bark. The oak was boiled and then cut into segments with a wedge. Finer, narrower bands of oak were also cut; these were trimmed with a spokeshave.

When working, the basket-maker kept his material moist to ensure pliancy. As he wove, the wood would set into the required shape. The strength of the cleft willow made the articles popular as shopping baskets.

COILED BASKETRY OR LIPE

Basket-making utilising straw rope was once in general use in Wales. Districts where ample supplies of straw were available used this type of coiled basketry in preference to any other. It was much in vogue in South-West Wales, and in especial in the Gower Peninsula. The more recent vogue for raffia work is reminiscent of the older craft of lipe; it depends, however, not on indigenous material but on imported goods.

The thickness of the straw depended on the purpose of the article being made. 'As thick as a man's forefinger', 'as thick as one's fist' were the rough calculations of rural areas. A dozen or more lengths of straw were smoothed out, sometimes moistened, and sometimes wrapped, to form the rope. Long lengths of strong straw were used for string. For large articles rods of green willow were inserted into the centre of the straw lengths for strengthening and to secure a good shape. Green withies were often used as handles for coiled straw baskets.

Straw furniture was a usual feature in the Welsh home. Truckle beds, which could be easily accommodated under an ordinary bed when not in use, were frequently made of straw. Chairs were made of coiled straw. Some were hooded. They were strong and durable, and were handed down as heirlooms. They were very warm. Bee-hives were made of skelp and straw work; there was a disadvantage in that the honey could not be easily removed from them. Seed lips, corn measures and baskets for storing meal, all made in lipe work, were usual on farms.

Akin to making baskets from straw was the art of making straw rope. It was made by means of twisting with a hook. A wet day was chosen for the work. Two people were occupied in the process. The ropes were used for tethering cattle to their stalls, and to secure hay and corn stacks.

GREEN WILLOW TRAPS

Unpeeled willow is used for making lobster pots, and eel and salmon traps. Willow rods are superior to wire and do not rot. The making of the basket-work traps has been traditional since the Middle Ages. It forms a spare-time occupation of people living on the Welsh coast.

These traps are characterised by strong individuality. The tech-nique of making them differs widely within a small radius. Tradition dies hard, and the creeks where the traps are used are often widely isolated from each other. Communication by land, as in older days, is often difficult, and in such isolation a local pattern tends to be-come established.

Fishermen make these traps for their own use, but occasionally one more dextrous than the others, or perhaps more diligent, makes them to sell. Crab and lobster pots are placed in the sea water, and the fishermen lift them each day and empty them as there is need. The traps give service over several seasons. They suffer less from their victims than from the onslaught of rough seas.

Local willow is often used and is plaited unpeeled. A dome shape, reminiscent of early beehives, is a favourite shape for lobster pots.

The fishing season extends from April to October, and so the trap is subject to long and continuous use. The height of an average pot is from two and a half to three feet. The willow rods bend inward at the top for about six inches. Bait is placed strategically on willow rods across the entrance of the trap. A cylindrical passage of closely woven basket leads into the trap, and an intricate arrangement of sharp rods makes any attempt at escape a real difficulty. Lobster pots are hung on strong ropes to which pieces of cork are attached.

Crab pots resemble lobster pots but they are not so high. The unpeeled willows, though often thin and having an appearance of frailty, are extremely strong.

Fish traps known as kiddles were extensively used in the Middle Ages. They proved so effective that regulations were introduced to control their use.

Wicker traps were used at the mouth of the Severn to catch salmon. A fish readjusted the balance of the trap as it entered and prevented its own escape. Some traps had a hoop of basket-work fitted within them. A number of sharply pointed stakes were fixed to the hoops. The fish could enter the trap easily, but exit was very difficult.

Eel traps known as 'wills' were used on the Severn. They were smaller than salmon traps. They were long cylinders of basket-work. Their life was shorter. They were used in fresh water, and their preservation by any chemical substance was ruled out, as the smell would make the trap ineffectual.

CORACLES

Basket-work is the foundation of coracles – those small, keel-less black boats still used in a few Welsh rivers even today. They were used by the early Britons, as is evidenced by old carvings, and by contemporary testimony. They have changed but little since the time when our early fore-fathers covered their basket boats with the skins of wild beasts, and rowed boldly into open seas to meet their enemies, and fight them with wooden spears tipped with fish-bone.

Giraldus Cambrensis described the coracles of Cenarth as he saw them in 1188. It is astonishing how realistic the description appears to anyone who has stood near the beautiful falls of the Teifi within recent times :

'The boats which they employ in fishing or in crossing the rivers are made of twigs, not oblong or pointed, but almost round, or rather triangular, covered both within and without with raw hides. When a salmon thrown into one of the boats strikes it hard with his tail, he often oversets it, and endangers both the vessel and its navigator. The fishermen, according to the custom of the country, in going to and from the rivers carry these boats on their shoulders; on which occasion that famous dealer in fables, Bled-dercus, who lived a little before our time, thus mysteriously said,

"There is amongst us a people who, when they go out in search
of their prey, carry their horses on their backs to the place of
plunder; in order to catch their prey they leap upon their
horses and when it is taken, carry their horses home again upon
their shoulders." '

These frail boats are very seaworthy, but they are used today mainly
on rivers. Though seen in diminishing numbers as fishing rights to
their owners are curtailed, they are still used on the rivers Towy,
Teifi, Dee and Severn, and a few other rivers. The original covering of hide has been replaced by canvas, which is waterproofed by
tar or pitch. According to the Irish legend of St Brendan, the
famous voyager, fifth-century sailors took fat or butter with them
on their journeys to protect the skin as need arose. Nowadays the
fishermen keeps a pot of boiling tar for repair work. When he takes
the coracle from the water, the fisherman turns his boat over and
weights it down with stones. When the coracle is dry its owner
carries it on his back in the fashion of a Red Indian with his canoe.
Llwyth dyn ei gorrwg – the weight of burden a man can carry is
the weight of his coracle – became a proverbial saying in Wales.

There are some slight divergencies in the shapes of coracles. Once
established, a type is seldom altered. The tradition of burning the
coracle on a heap of straw with full funeral rights when its owner
died may have, in an indirect way, ensured the continuance of the
craft of making the coracle. The right to ply a coracle on a river
was usually hereditary. The four-man coracle seems to have passed
out of existence, and the one-man coracle is superseding the two-
man type. 'A man and his coracle are one in a storm' is an old
saying.

The lightness of the coracle is one of its prominent features. A
big craft seldom weighs more than fifteen pounds; smaller craft
weigh as little as seven to eight pounds. Measurements vary; six
feet in length and about four feet wide are average measurements.
The bottom of the boat is flat, and is about four feet square. The
sides of the boat rise perpendicularly from the bottom. It is seldom
more than a foot deep. One end of the boat is pointed, the point
being blunted in some localities. Severn coracles have a 'waisted'
appearance, being drawn in towards the centre in curves. This gives
the boat two compartments. Coracles on the Teifi are smaller than
those on the Towy, and their ends are less rounded.

The original covering of a coracle appears to have been a cow-hide, the measurements of which pre-determined the small size of the boat. The tradition of a small boat has been maintained although the covering is now tarred canvas. Partly because of its small dimensions the craft is suitable for use on lakes and rivers. The Irish *curragh*, which in some ways resembles the Welsh *corwgl*, is a keeled boat which can with greater safety travel in open sea.

BASKETRY TECHNIQUE

The basket-maker uses few tools. He uses knives and also shears and a rapping iron for pressing the rods closely together. He uses lead weights to secure good shapes in round baskets, and he some-times uses a simple screw clasp when making the bases of square baskets. He depends mainly on his bare hands for the work, and on the 'feel' of his material, a fact that becomes the more evident when we remember the dexterity of the blind in this particular craft. He usually works seated, sometimes on the floor of an outhouse, for his materials tend to create an untidy litter. For ease in working, he often rests his basket on a sloping plank.

When making a round basket he concentrates first on the frame-work of the base. When the main rods have been 'criss-crossed' they are interwoven with thinner rods. Strong rods are thrust at intervals into the woven circumference, and here are bent upwards to form the sides of the basket. Thin rods are interwoven between these, and the border is plaited. Rectangular baskets are made on a framework of strong willow rods. Handles are added.

To ensure ease in manufacturing, the basket-maker soaks his rods before using them. There are special terms for the various types of interweaving. A single weave is called randing; two or more rods interwoven form slewing. When two rods are intertwined in the same direction the term used is pairing. If the worker uses three rods he is waling. These terms are familiar on the Welsh border in the old basket-maker's song:

> I can rand at your command
> Put on a decent border
> Upset right, wale alright
> And keep my stakes in order.

The basket-maker's range was a wide one covering market baskets, fruit baskets, hampers and baskets for poultry.

Furniture for both indoor and outdoor use was made of basketry; and babies' cradles, as early manuscripts testify, have been made from wicker from the twelfth century onwards. The willow rods plaited together form light durable articles that can be easily cleaned.

The country basket-maker, working often in leisure time, is content to go searching for his osiers. He cuts the rods in the spring, arranging them in bundles and binding them with a strip of willow. The bundles are stocked in the open. If the rods are to be used for white work they are stood in water for a month or two. Sometimes the basket-maker will make a special pit for them to stand in. He sets great store on this preliminary work, for attention to it ensures that his rods will be pliant, that they will peel easily, and that they will be cleanly white.

Certain rods are boiled. The bundle of osiers is immersed in the boiler, and the rods or 'buffs', as these boiled rods are called, are subject to long boiling. The buffs are stronger than the peeled rods. After boiling, they are left in the open to dry.

A two-pronged fork is used for peeling. The rods are then sorted out in sizes.

Green willow is also collected; it is kept for special work.

RUSH AND SEA-GRASS WORK

Rush work is a country craft which has flourished in Wales since the Middle Ages. Prior to that, rushes were used as floor coverings in cottage and in hall.

The flowering rush (*Juncus effusius*) is common on marshy ground, bordering on rivers, lakes and ponds.

There is a distinct art in gathering rushes. They are cut as closely as possible to their roots. They are tied in bundles or bolts, and the stems are kept vertical. They are dried thoroughly in the wind and kept away from strong light.

When they are to be used, however, they are dampened carefully and protected from too much moisture.

Floor mats and table mats are made in a chequerboard pattern by intertwining the rushes. The general shape of the finished article, square or oval, is pre-determined by the initial centre pattern.

Children in rural areas of Wales often amused themselves by making toys of woven rush. Rattles and cages were made of the strong and pliant reeds and designs were traditional. Country labourers amused themselves in like manner, making intricate and ornamental cockades for their own hats, and for the manes of their horses. They also made knots for the baskets of the girls they favoured.

Work in rush is still practised. It is often very fine. The designs bear a close affinity with those that adorn early Celtic crosses.

'As a designer myself, I am convinced that much intricate Celtic strap work such as the Book of Kells, or the boulder designs of the Stone Crosses, were based on the patterns used in green rush or sea-grass work. These green and pliant materials would be much more common at a period when corn was scarce and straw was kept for fodder; frequently in those days the grass was allowed to grow up along the long stubble and mowed together with it. In the natural weave of rush and sea-grass, the turns, though abrupt, are slightly rounded, and while green, the spiral follows a very constant curve. Straw is hollow and cylindrical, and so will always flatten in plait and crack in turning, if the angle is sharp. Thus we find a marked contrast between the English plait and the curving Celtic scroll.' (Dorothy Hartley, *Made in England*.)

The strap designs are clearly evident in the rush seats given to stools. These are a common sight in a typical Welsh kitchen, and they are now promoted to a status of pride in modern furnishing. The natural brown rush allied to oak and beech frames makes objects of beauty. The ornament is there in the strap pattern, but the aesthetic value is subservient to the functional. The stool used in modest daily service is simple, and yet it is far more pleasing than furniture which is more exclusive and ornate. The stool is evidence of a proper use of materials; there is a fittingness in their use. The craftsmanship which goes into the making of the stool is born of skill, knowledge and experience, giving to the whole a lasting value.

Antiquity of design is often linked with antiquity of material. Civilised man, like his early ancestors, has tended to make use of products close at hand. Rush and sea-grass are plentiful in Wales. Consequently men and women in early Celtic settlements made use of them to cover their houses, and to turn them into mats and screens to adorn their homes, much in the manner of today.

Sea-reed – *mor-hesg* – grows in abundance in certain regions of the Welsh coast. Its importance has been traditional on the west coast of Anglesey. Great stretches of marram grass bind the sand near the villages of Aberffraw, Rhosneigr and Newborough. The people of Anglesey recognised its worth, for it flourished in regions where the more usual grasses or trees would not grow. E. A. Lewis in *The Mediaeval Boroughs of Snowdonia* refers to a custom in force in Newborough which forbade the cutting of *moreaske rush* in an area extending for two miles from the borough. The grass was sown to protect the low-lying land from the strong tidal waves. This was abandoned and the marram grass alone appears to have served as a natural defence from the encroachment of sand and of sea.

The use of sea-grass in craftsmanship must have been almost contemporaneous with its growth on the *twyni* or sand dunes of the west coast. When a rush industry was established in Anglesey in the nineteenth century, designs and techniques drew strength from those which were traditional in the area. It was about the year 1835 that the crafts of making mats, nets and ropes from the *mor-hesg* became organised.

It was a whole-time or a seasonal occupation. Women were engaged in it while the men worked in the fields. As an organised craft, it was not practised throughout the island, but was localised in centres in the west, more particularly around Newborough. Here again, as with so many rural crafts, the work was often hereditary. Outsiders were looked at askance. The work of novices was frowned upon and stress was laid on the imperative need of learning the art of plaiting before one entered one's 'teens. Thus was ensured a 'closed-shop' of sea-grass workers.

The marram grass was harvested at the end of summer. By custom, each woman went to a particular sand dune and garnered her crop of *mor-hesg*. Her right was sure though unwritten, and could be compared to that which directed the path of her fellow country woman to gather cockles at Penclawdd on the Gower coast.

Special care was given to the harvesting of the marram grass. Each worker knew the necessity of good material for her wares. She waded through the sand carrying a special bill-hook, fitted with a heavy head made by a local blacksmith. The grass was long – often as long as three feet – and the roots lay deep beneath the shifting surface of the sand. Each woman endeavoured to cut the grass near its roots, thus ensuring a good length. The grass was arranged in bundles, and then spread out to 'win'. This meant that it was treated much like hay laid out to dry. It was also stacked much in the manner of hay, and bound with a length of marram grass. A skilled hand was required to stack the moist and slippery grass. The stacks were kept in the open for about a month, and were then transferred to an outhouse. In this way each worker gathered the material that she herself intended to use in the winter. Sometimes bundles of marram grass were bought at centres such as Aberffraw. This, however, was not usual, save among older women. The grass was sold in bundles, and the usual price was a shilling for a bundle of four or five pounds.

Sea-grass was considered particularly suitable for making mats. The usual method was by plaiting, and the finished article bore a close resemblance to the type of mat usually associated with the craftwork of primitive tribes in Africa. Considerable dexterity was shown in the plaiting process. Each craftswoman took a bundle of sea-grass numbering six or seven strands; she knocked out all tangles by beating it against her knee. Taking about six of these bunches she plaited a strip approximately four inches wide. She plaited with her right hand, and inserted new strands as they were needed with her left hand. The beginning of the plait was fastened to a leather loop hung from the ceiling. A heavy stone or poker served as a weight at the end of a finished plait. The right side of the strip was smooth, but the left side, where new strands had been inserted, was rough. Most women worked individually in their homes and at intervals in their housework. Young women tended to group together in teams of five or six; they worked in some empty outhouse where the litter made by the sea-grass did not interfere with household organisation. Work under such conditions was congenial. Each woman sat at her work and plaited at about shoulder height.

The left hand strengthened the plait as it proceeded. When a strip of about 80 yards had been made, it was rolled into a ball and stored away. When many strips had been prepared, they were sewn together into a mat. The sewing was done with a packing needle; a thread was made by twisting together three or four grasses. Sewing the strips together side by side was tedious work, and also more cumbersome than the plaiting process. Mats measuring approximately three feet by nine were made. Their sewing demanded considerably more space for the worker than the process of plaiting.

Thatching mats and also horticultural mats were also made. The use of the thatching mat was originally regarded as temporary; it was to serve as a covering and protection from the weather until such time as the farmer could cover his crop with a direct covering of thatch.

But in actual use the virtues of the sea-grass mat became apparent. Just as straw thatching is regarded as superior to a corrugated roof, so too is a marram grass mat considered superior to a direct thatch on a standing crop. It was recognised as being a sure protection from rain; its open weave allowed for a greater current of air than thatch; further, it was found that under sea-grass mats the crops never heated.

Horticulturalists as well as agriculturalists favoured sea-grass mats. Consequently the Anglesey workers prepared mats for garden and store-room use. Long, narrow mats measuring about twelve feet by four feet were made. Smaller mats were made for strawberry beds; gardeners valued them as they kept the fruit clean and free from slugs.

Grass ropes were also made. Sea-grass was used; bundles of it were twisted by hand. It was much in demand for the packing of fragile articles, such as glass and pottery. Another interesting use was as a covering for barbed wire.

The economic conditions that lay behind the rush mat industry in Anglesey in the nineteenth century have been fully described in *Rural Industries of England and Wales*, Volume IV, by A. M. Jones. All trading was done on the barter system. She writes:

'There was no co-operation among makers, and all trade was done by barter. Each worker made her purchases at the grocer's and butcher's shop giving the shopkeeper as many mats in payment. These the shopkeeper stored until local merchants came round in early summer to buy them. The local merchants took the mats to the fairs held in July in Criccieth, and Pwllheli, and here the farmers would buy their annual stock of mats. As a rule the worker was given food to the value of one shilling and tenpence for each mat, and the shopkeeper sold them for about three shillings. Thus the shopkeeper made a profit both on the mats and the food given in exchange to the mat maker. If the worker had a little stock of money, she paid for her provisions in cash, and kept her mats to sell to the merchant direct, thus realizing the profit that would otherwise go to the shopkeeper. But few had money to do this.

'The grass ropes which were sold mostly to the railway company were also very poorly paid for. Thus the women, many of whom were entirely dependent on this source of income, found it very difficult to eke out a living.'

The Newborough Mat Makers Association was set up to improve conditions. Financial transactions took the place of barter. The wares of the mat makers were advertised on a wide scale, and the efforts of the Association, based on a co-operative foundation, yielded good results.

Sea reed was also used for the making of besoms. The *mor-hesg* was harvested and dried as for the making of mats. Sea-reed brushes were used for lime-washing the walls of the houses. They were particularly useful for this purpose as lime tends to burn the finer bristles of better brushes. The sea-reed brushes were cheap and easily replaced. To make a brush a wooden handle had a hole cut in it. A bunch of marram grass was passed through it. The ends were secured beneath the opening in the handle by a length of grass.

In making besoms, bunches of reeds are tied securely around a broomstick. The ends are bent back from the stick and tied again. These besoms are inferior to those made from birch, yet many favour them. They are quickly made, and the worker who makes them as occasional work can sell them easily in the neighbourhood, or in bulk to an ironmonger.

CORN DOLLIES

Winifred Newton-Sealey of Stoke Edith on the Welsh border, has achieved an international reputation as a straw plaiter and maker of corn dollies. The interest in creating the straw dollies, a relic of a ritual primitive past, is strong. She is called on to demonstrate her craft in festivals and shows and agricultural exhibitions, and now conducts residential courses to meet an enthusiastic demand.

By tradition, corn dollies are made from corn grown locally. Corn is a generic name for a plant producing grain : wheat, oats, barley, rye. Wheat straw is usual for corn dollies. Winter-sown wheat has a thick stalk and large head; that sown in the spring has a more regularly-shaped stalk which is much thinner.

The straw plaiter takes pride in cutting his own corn. There is an exact time for cutting – the moment when it turns from green to gold. A specialist knows the best corn for his craft, long from the ear to the first joint, unstained with damp, hollow in the stalk, and with an even head, and golden in colour when dried. Standing wheat is reckoned to be the best. There is a preference for spring wheat for it has a small well-shaped head and thinner stalk. Winter wheat is reserved for decoration. The straw-plaiter devoted to his craft will plant his own corn, will care for it and will harvest it. By modern farming methods, corn is often sprayed with chemical manures; as a result the stalks are often short and solid.

Corn dollies feature prominently in church and farm decorations at harvest time. Legend and mythology are interwoven in the straw symbols. They were made to honour Ceres, the Earth Mother. In times past a farmer would leave a row of wheat standing in the fields at harvest time to ensure good luck in the future. The goddess Ceres was supposed to dwell in this sheaf. To placate her, an idol was made of straw. The word 'idol' was corrupted to 'dolly'. The last stalks of corn were fashioned into the figure of a woman. It was preserved carefully until seed was sown in the spring.

The custom dates back into antiquity; when corn was first cultivated in lands east of the Mediterranean, men made corn dollies, fashioning intricate straw plaitings with stiff work-hardened hands. They, too, believed that the spirit of Ceres slept in the last ears of corn; it would rest in the dolly until the following year. Then the dolly would be flung over the ploughed fields, or maybe it would be added to the corn seed, to ensure another golden harvest.

The dolly takes on different forms in different districts. Corn dollies proper range from small figures to tall corn maidens. Traditional specimens include angels, spirals, 'Welsh' fans, harvest and country designs.

Away from the ritualistic and symbolic, the straw plaiter has a wide scope, fashioning babies' rattles, umbrellas, lanterns, shepherds' crooks, spinning wheels, bells, pipes, pitchforks. A further development in the craft of straw work is its alliance with dried flower pictures and wall decorations, fire screens and models, often placed under Victorian glass domes.

The Knark or Nik dolly is a favourite. It too takes on different forms in different localities. It is associated with harvest rituals of primitive peoples in Asia Minor. It is made from a solid column of straw, and it is usually made with a five-straw plait. The Drop Dolly is more intricate; here the figure is hollow.

In some districts there has been a deviation from the human

figure. A Celtic straw cross, sometimes known as the Bridget Cross, associated with Ireland, is customary.

A further deviation is a 'countryman's favour'. These became associated with the workmanship of village youths on a Sunday evening after the busy work of harvesting. They were made with two- to six-straw plaits, and were trimmed with hedgerow flowers, nuts and berries.

7

Metal

PEDOLWR • DAI MORGAN (Y GOF) • FARRIER

SMITHCRAFT

Gethin Williams is the village blacksmith in the delightful rural village of *Llanarthney, in the vale of Towy.* His son, Ken, assists him, maintaining the family craft. He too is a very proficient blacksmith, and he had help from C.O.S.I.R.A. with the training.

They have plenty of work shoeing horses. They make their own horseshoes at the forge. Gethin Williams has worked steadily for 30 years as a shoeing smith. They have branched out to create gates, fire-irons and grates, intricately decorated and some bearing animal heads. Specialised work of this nature has brought orders from all over Britain, and many export orders. Special effort went into the creation of an ornate crest, commissioned by the Royal Automobile Club, and now placed over the main gates in Pall Mall, London. The men's work is its own recommendation, but any difficulties have been eased away by the Welsh Guild of Wrought Ironworkers, which among other things helps craftsmen to find markets.

O. *John Roger Thomas*, blacksmith and wrought-iron worker *of Tumble, near Llanelli*, is an expert in metal work. In this age of plastic and concrete, he has inherited his craft from his father, Mr. Will Thomas, a colliery blacksmith, and is devoted to preserving one of the most ancient rural crafts.

Economic security is achieved by being a blacksmith and farrier. Mr. Thomas is however a creative craftsman. He has the ability to turn iron into a thing of beauty. His designs range from simple candlesticks to elaborate fire screens and ornamental gates for cottage or hall. The Council for Small Industries in Rural Areas held a Wrought-Iron and Ornamental Work Exhibition in London. A special exhibit made by Roger Thomas, a five-branch candelabra, made in wrought iron, was chosen for display.

At *Talsarn, in Dyfed*, the firm of *Messrs. Price* has a remarkably high reputation in smithcraft and in farriery. It also has the distinction of having the only registered woman blacksmith in Britain.

The blacksmith who specialises in shoeing and repairing remains among the most flourishing of the older craftsmen. Primarily, he is occupied with the shoeing of horses. The keen interest in pony-trekking throughout Wales has meant increased and steady trade for blacksmiths. In the smithy, ploughs, harrows and farm implements are made, and more often, repaired. The blacksmith often works in conjunction with some other craftsman such as the carpenter who, in turn, supplies him with tool handles. A blacksmith often acquires a high reputation for making some particular implement, such as a hay lifter, a shovel, or a patented plough.

The blacksmith who has a knowledge of farriery, and who has skill in the management of horses, is a craftsman indeed. Efficient shoeing demands specialised anatomical knowledge. The skill of the blacksmith lies in the accuracy of his eye, as well as in the strength of his arm. He is, of necessity, a quick worker; he dispenses with plans. The wise farmer patronises the same blacksmith, for the skilled craftsman grows conscious of the idiosyncracies of a particular horse. Moreover, he develops an astonishingly accurate idea of what shoe will fit a horse he is accustomed to attending.

Most smiths prepare shoes in readiness, thus saving time when a horse is brought to the door. The iron bars are cut to special lengths; after forging, the shoe is shaped so as to be comfortable in wear and serviceable on the road surface. The shape of the shoe varies with the type of horse, and also with the type of work to which it is subjected. Wedge-shaped sockets, capable of retaining the nails after the shoe has worn down, are inserted in the shoe. An efficient blacksmith pays particular heed to the condition of the hoof when fitting a shoe.

A knowledge of farriery adds considerably to the reputation of a blacksmith. The letters R.S.S. over a smithy door, show that he is a shoeing smith, and a member of the Worshipful Company of Farriers.

A smithy is nowadays one of the busiest workshops in the countryside. Modern farms are dependent on agricultural machinery, which, working at high speed, are subject to great strain. Even their temporary breakdown is a great expense to the farmer, and so he welcomes a smithy close at hand which is able to repair metal. Thanks to the installation of welding plants, some smithies are able to make, on the premises, new parts for agricultural machinery.

We have only to consider the many tools used in husbandry to realise how vitally necessary is the craft of the smith, even in the most remote valley of the Principality. The shepherd on the lonely Welsh hills has always turned to the smith as an ally. He marked his flock with the aid of marking irons fashioned by the smith. These carried an initial, sometimes two, and also a traditional mark – a particularly important characteristic in a country where patronymics are few. The marking irons were made with the intention of wearing well. They were in annual use, and were subject to hard wear, being inserted into a pot full of boiling tar or pitch before being applied. The smith also created the shepherd's crook, attaching it to a long pole of ash. The skilled craftsman gave consideration to the pecularities of the shepherd's flock. He fashioned the crook in such a way, and set it at such an angle, that the shepherd could with ease hook a recalcitrant sheep by its hind leg, confident in the knowledge that the slot was adequate for the insertion of the leg without damage. Just as the carpenter of mediaeval times could ease the burden of the ox by making a wooden yoke that was smooth and easy, so could the smith ensure comfort for the sheep with skilful fashioning of the crook.

The hedger down in the valley was likewise dependent on the smith. The craftsmen made billhooks, specially designed for forearm cutting. According to local needs, they were made in narrow or broad proportions, and fitted with long or short handles. The local stamp or design of many a tool is an indication of a skilled smith's foresight, and understanding of the needs of the worker.

The Iron Age denotes no special period in universal chronology, but among each race it indicates a culture which is marked by a knowledge of the art of iron making and consequently of the general employment of iron implements.

Iron was manufactured by the Celts at an early date. The Teutons derived their name for iron from the Celts, and this may infer their first acquaintance with the metal itself. Celts on the Continent are reputed to have used iron broadswords at the battle of Anio in the 4th century B.C. It is believed that iron was worked in Sussex by the Britons in the time of Julius Caesar. Likewise, it is believed that the ships of Caesar were inferior to those of the Britons and their allies in North-Western France, for the oak timbers of the Celtic ships were riveted together with iron pins as 'thick as a man's thumb'. Furthermore, the Celts used iron chains instead of the primitive rope cables used by the Romans.

The mediaeval smith was an honoured member of the community. The old Welsh laws show that he was a person of high prestige in the King's Court. He received his land free. He had the right to use the King's mill. His revenues included the feet of the cattle in the King's Court, and also the heads. He received four pence from each slave he set at liberty from chains. He had the right to claim beer and mead from the royal vessels.

Outstanding among the Welsh smiths of the eighteenth century were Robert and John Davies of Wrexham, sons of a famous smith father, Huw Davies. The father's skilled work is thought to include the chancel gates at the parish church at Wrexham. The craftwork is much in keeping with fifteenth- and sixteenth-century work. When the smith took it on himself to create ornamentation, he did so much in the manner of that produced by the wood carver, who went to nature for his inspiration. Ironwork gates and screens were used extensively in the sixteenth and in the seventeenth centuries.

They were ideal vehicles for skilled ornamentation. Huw Davies, working at Efail y Groes Foel, Bersham, set an inspiring example to his sons Robert and John. Their work radiated from Wrexham in all directions to enhance manor houses and churches in North Wales, and on the Welsh border. The high standard of craftsmanship achieved by the Davies Brothers places them on a par with Jean Tijou, the famous craftsman of the reign of William and Mary, who brought into prominence a French style, and whose ironwork was lavishly decorated. Their work may be compared favourably too with the most famous smiths of the first half of the eighteenth century, men such as Edney of Bristol, Bakewell of Derbyshire, and Thomas Robinson.

As the manor house increased in comfort, it became less and less a fortress. Decorative iron gates with their attendant railings screened parks and pleasure gardens from the high road. The gates became the province of the smith. Herein the Davies brothers excelled, for they created some of the finest work ever produced by Welsh craftsmen.

Among the many beautiful gates attributed to them are those at Carden Hall, Malpas, Cheshire; the gates and railings at Plas Erddig, Wrexham; the gates of Abbey House, Shrewsbury; and the gates of the churches at Wrexham, Oswestry and Ruthin. Other gates attributed to them are at Chirk Castle, Denbighshire; at Coedllai, Mold; Mere Hall, Droitwich, and Powis Castle. There is little that can compare with the work of the Davies smiths in Wales, or indeed in Britain. Describing the gates at Plas Erddig, one writer states that they are 'the richest example of wrought-iron railings existing in Britain'. There is a belief that the gates were made originally for Stantsey Park, and that they were removed to Plas Erddig before the First World War. Design and workmanship have unmistakable features of Davies craft. Great scrolls form the crest of the gates, and they are of such proportions that they could be carried by railings twice the dimensions of the existing supports.

The White Gates at Leaswood Hall, Mold, rank among the great smithing achievements of the country. Details of design and of workmanship are truly wonderful. The Black Gates are on the road to Mold. To the top of the overthrow, they stand 20 feet high. They stand at the entrance to the park, and have much in common with the White Gates. Together, the gates are known locally as Heaven and Hell. The fret patterns on the piers of the gates resemble those at Eaton Hall, and give support to the claim that all are by the Davies brothers. There is some doubt concerning the authorship of the Malpas Gates. Robert Davies died in 1749, and John in 1755, and the Malpas Gates in details and design reveal characteristics of a decade or two later. And yet a trained eye can detect a close affinity between the Malpas Gates and those of Wrexham Church.

TOOLSMITH

Eric Cartledge is the last remaining independent toolsmith in Britain. His skills are hereditary. They have been handed down in the family for three generations. He is a toolsmith at *Overton-on-Dee near Ruabon*. He makes tools – especially fine ones – for delicate work. He specialises in fine-nosed pliers. These are used for work in intricate circuitry in radio and television sets, and for meticulous work such as setting stones in jewellery. Because big manufacturers absorbed small privately-owned manufacturing plants, few toolsmiths were able to compete. The high cost of overheads intensified the problem, and unless more independent toolsmiths establish themselves, it is unlikely that the craft will survive.

JAPAN WARE OF PONTYPOOL

Japan Ware of Pontypool and of Usk, so greatly sought after by the collectors of today, had an international reputation. Historically, the life of the craft and industry was short. It did not develop out of the needs of national life. It left behind no living traditions. Nevertheless, its appeal is still strong. Its prosperity impinged on the lives of the workers in the industrial valleys of Monmouthshire (Gwent). It contributed to the development of the prosperous tin-plate industry in its early stages. Its craftsmen can claim a worthy place among those who practised in Wales.

It owed its inspiration to John Allgood of Northamptonshire, who had settled about the year 1860 in Pontypool, where he conducted experiments in the by-products of coal at the iron works at Capel Hanbury.

At this time lacquer enjoyed a high reputation in Britain. In the later Stuart period it was used to decorate furniture and personal accessories. Oriental processes were expensive, for they required as many as thirty or more coatings. A sham lacquer achieved with copal varnish was sometimes used. This was superseded by a Japanese hard varnish. Thus the craft obtained its name of Japanning. The lacquered articles were decorated with gold and coloured paints.

John Allgood, engaged in experiments with bituminous coal, alighted on a method of varnishing which could be applied under heat, not only to wood but to metal. Therein lay its superiority, according to Allgood's mind, for lacquering of metal would, he held, be of more enduring worth.

Several years of experimentation followed. At length, Allgood had the satisfaction of achieving a varnish which, when applied with colour and heated, took on itself a close resemblance to the finest oriental lacquer. Content with the quality of this lacquer, Allgood found himself baffled by the nature of the metal available for use. However meticulous his applications of the lacquer, it showed itself irregular on the rough surface of the iron plates to which it was applied.

Edward, John Allgood's son, continued the work of industrial experiment on the death of his father. His processing of the metal resulted in rolled tin-plate. Iron sheets were tinned, and the Welsh tin-plate industry developed. The iron works at Pontypool were near the Forest of Dean, whence came a special type of iron peculiarly suited to tin-plating.

Japanning was known elsewhere. Factories in South Staffordshire, the main rivals to Pontypool, lacked, however, the knowledge acquired by Allgood concerning the perfecting of tin-plates.

Edward Allgood, secure in his success, opened about the year 1720 what came to be known as the Pontypool Japan Works, at the bottom of Trusnant, a suburb of Pontypool. Fastidiously careful work characterised the industry from the first. Detailed attention was given to the tin-plate. A thin even covering of Cornish tin was applied to the plates. The South Staffordshire Japanners primed their plates, but were confronted with cracks and peeled surfaces in their finished work. The Pontypool workers showed a superiority in their varnish too. They mixed their colours, not with oil, but with a white varnish – an ingredient whose formula was a closely guarded secret.

Under Edward Allgood's leadership the work flourished. It is remarkable how wide and how excellent was the output at Pontypool, considering that the work was essentially done on a domestic basis. The workshops were small. They formed the upper storey of a small cottage, and the fittings of the workroom were few. The

Allgood family supplied the workers; they were supplemented by a small local work force. It is significant that the foreman was referred to as 'the garret master'. Out-workers, working in their own homes, decorated the ware.

Originality of design was fostered, but certain stock motifs soon gained ascendancy. At first there were standard borders referred to as 'die-punched patterns, interspersed with blank intervals'. With the ever-broadening custom of tea-drinking, tea-trays and tea-tables hammered from thinly rolled tin-plate, became fashionable. Pontypool lace-edged trays with tortoise-shell centres became equally the vogue. They formed a fine substitute for the beautifully lacquered wood trays brought to Wales in sailing vessels from the Orient. The tortoise-shell background was reminiscent of the Staffordshire pottery of the time, and became in due course a characteristic of Pontypool Japan Ware.

Sometimes a plain background was introduced. Sprays of flowers or fruit were painted on these backgrounds, coming out into distinct highlights on one side, and fading to nothingness on the other. With characteristic care, painstaking methods were applied in order to achieve the naturalness and brilliance of the flowers. Simple line-work in gilt added to the charm of many designs. Most characteristic of all motifs – at Usk as well as at Pontypool – were the painted butterflies that decorated the Japanned articles. The prevalence of the painted butterflies gave the pseudonym of butterflies – *pila-pala Pontypool* – to the residents of the two towns. Another phrase which gained currency was *As round as a Pontypool waiter*, a waiter being one of the round trays, which developed almost grotesque proportions as the 1780's advanced.

Articles of Pontypool ware were numerous; they included canisters, candlesticks, comb trays, urns, tea-pots, letter racks, toast racks, and similar articles, and at times, ingenious novelties. Edward Allgood, who inherited his father's business acumen, continued to direct the work. To him goes the credit for the majority of the stock designs at Pontypool. Border and band patterns appear to have been his speciality. His introduction of line, including the waving stormont line, seemed to enhance the more intricate centre designs.

When the Pontypool Japan Works passed into the hands of Edward's sons there was a division of interest. Thomas Allgood remained at Pontypool; his two brothers moved seven miles away to Usk, where they set up a factory in opposition. The family secret relating to the white varnish and its tradition was kept; what was perhaps more important was the degree of exactitude concerning every stage of work in the creation of Pontypool ware. Rivalry between the factories at Pontypool and Usk resulted in an advance in decoration and in style.

There is written evidence by way of old account books of the prosperity of the enterprise. There were agents for Japanned ware in many parts of the country. Names of purchasers and prices indicate the high value set on the ware: 'An Oval Tray with a Landskipp made for Sir Charles Morgan – 15 guineas; An Oval Tray damaged, sold to a Quaker – £4. 10s. 0d.' Such items, however, represented the more costly ware. Cheaper articles were made, and these were sold by ironmongers and shops stocking fancy ware.

The firm at Pontypool came to be known as Allgood and Company. It prospered, and additional workers were introduced into the family enterprise.

There was a close bond between artist and craftsman in this stage of the evolution of industrial democracy. The foreman decorator was Benjamin Barker. He was a travelling artist who specialised in sporting subjects. He settled in Pontypool, where were born his two sons, destined to become themselves artists of considerable repute. Thomas and Benjamin Barker, later of Bath, assisted their father in the decoration of some of the most attractive Pontypool Japanned ware. Thomas painted shepherds and shepherdesses set against a rustic background; Benjamin (junior) specialised in landscapes.

A high standard of craftsmanship was maintained in the small towns of Wales in the late eighteenth century. Edward Allgood had no monopoly of Japanning tin-plate. A London firm achieved a high reputation, and had the distinction of supplying Japanned ware of high quality to the King. Yet Pontypool, though a small and in some ways a remote town, could produce ware superior to that of the metropolis.

'Welsh lacquer' achieved continental fame. The international repute was fostered under the new director, William – 'Old Billy' – Allgood, who inherited a share in the factory on the death of his father in 1776. For the next 37 years, under his directorship, the work expanded. Artist-copiers were supplemented by local tinsmiths who worked in their homes under the supervision of a foreman.

Aware of the rivalry of Birmingham Japanners, who sold their ware more cheaply, 'Old Billy' is reputed to have challenged them to a test. This was reminiscent of mediaeval days, taking the form of 'ordeal by fire'. Pontypool ware could stand the test. It emerged unimpaired from the heart of a charcoal fire. As a number of articles Japanned at Pontypool were used in conjunction with fire – tea and coffee urns, chestnut servers, kettles and the like – the reputation of the products was enhanced.

Rivalry between Usk and Pontypool led to the development in style of the latter. Favoured by such patrons as Louis XVI of France and the Duke of Wellington, 'Old Billy' Allgood aimed at a refinement of style which would bring his wares into keeping with the most elegant accessories of his time. Cleverly-designed moulds were introduced into the works for making tea urns and vases. They were fitted with mouldings of brass and bases of lead. Vessels intended for hot liquids had linings of copper.

Improvements were made in stoving, alterations being made in temperatures and in the time given to annealing. Following the eighteenth-century taste for topography, designs showed castles and landscapes. Lace-patterned borders now appeared in silver rather than gilt. The many colours introduced into the designs took upon themselves a more sombre effect, a result fostered by means of increased stoving. A mellow patina was introduced into the finished work by the use of a special varnish. Under 'Old Billy' Allgood, the Japanned ware at Pontypool acquired an excellence which it never later surpassed. Through its excellence of form and of design, orders came from all parts of Britain, from Holland and from France.

The exquisite lustre of the Pontypool ware was achieved at great cost. 'Old Billy' Allgood, incensed at the imitation from Wolverhampton traded as 'fancy Pontypool ware', claimed that his products were subjected to a process which involved their annealing for as many as 16 times. The quality of his wares was, of course, far superior to that of his imitators. The price of Pontypool ware by comparison seemed exorbitant. 'Old Billy' was to see his enterprise suffer as a result, and after his death the work, under the care of his widow, declined. Finally, in the second decade of the nineteenth century, it closed, and the workers who remained transferred their labours to Usk.

Among them was John Hughes, who was closely associated with the Allgood family. After many vicissitudes, the works passed into the control of a relative of the Allgoods, an Evan Jones, known familiarly as 'Old Ianto'.

Workers at Usk endeavoured to keep ahead of the times. They dispensed with the decorating of tin-plate, and imported articles – the then fashionable papier mâché from the South Midlands. This ensured cheaper products, and the workers adhered to the traditional patterns of pierced borders, scroll, flower and leaf motifs. Moreover, they Japanned the papier mâché motifs with the customary golden brown backgrounds, as opposed to the black background favoured in the Midland factories. To an extraordinary degree, the Japanners at Usk succeeded in their effort to achieve, in their decorative work, an imitation of inlaid gold or silver.

The hey-day of Usk ware was comparatively brief. It had to compete with factories that made imitations of their wares, and also with the ubiquitous tin-ware stencilled in bright patterns. With the death of 'Old Ianto' in 1860, the Usk factory closed. Until its sale in 1884 it had largely been a family concern, first in the kin of the Allgoods, and then in the family of Evan Jones. Until 1884 the Allgood secret formula for Japanning had been passed down orally, and there is no record of it ever having been made public.

CLOCK-MAKING

Alan Venables of Newtown, Powys, is a pioneer as well as a skilled craftsman. He has made what is in all probability the first Welsh barometer. He has created another innovation; a barometer set in leather. Clocks are also made in this setting. Of special appeal is his sunflower clock, surrounded by leather petals. It measures two feet, tip to tip and its movement is in quartz. Clocks are made in various styles. Some can be used with barometers to make a matching pair.

His craft has been a venture of faith and hard work. When he became redundant in the electronics industry he faced serious problems and challenges. He and his wife decided to stay in Mid-Wales, and to practise a craft which interested him. With minimal capital, he ventured into clock-making, in which he had always been interested. His venture started in his own garage, but in less than two years he has moved into a new workshop, the ground floor of an old flannel mill in Newtown. He is now exporting his work to various parts of the world.

The barometer with Welsh signs has authentic Celtic lettering.

An English translation is provided. Despite the fact that the barometer has for generations been almost indispensable to the farming and fishing folk of Wales, there is no evidence that they have ever been able to buy a barometer with the wording in their own tongue. The Welsh barometer is made not only in a leather case, but also with a wooden or slate frame made by Welsh craftsmen.

In the ranges of clocks no two are quite alike in detail and colour. Each, as an individual masterpiece, is numbered and signed.

In order to ensure supreme accuracy, quartz movements are fitted so that they will keep time to within a minute over a full year on a single battery.

Such has been the response to the craft produced by Alaven Designs, that its future appears to indicate *hindda* – set fair.

The Welsh as a nation have a strong peasant tradition; they are closely linked with the occupations associated with the soil and the sea. The sun and the seasons were the natural markers of time. It is somewhat surprising, therefore, to realise that, from an early stage, clocks were in comparatively general use in Wales. The Welshman in late mediaeval times may well have been familiar, not only with sundials, but also with clocks made in brass.

Dr I. Peate (*Clocks and Clock Making in Wales*) points out that although clocks were the perquisites of the wealthy in the fifteenth and sixteenth centuries, the Welsh poet, Lewis Glyn Cothi, makes reference to *y cloc bach* – possibly a lantern clock, by which he worked out a genealogical tree.

A tradition of clock-making may have been fostered in Wales, for when clockmakers organised themselves into a Worshipful Company in the City of London, in 1631, Welsh clockmakers were of sufficient standing to be accorded membership. The names of Welshmen are frequent in the records of the Company up to the nineteenth century.

Prominent among these names was that of William Hughes of Anglesey, who was made an honorary freeman of the Company in 1781. Dr Peate records how he made a musical automatic watch for the Emperor of China.

'It is six to nine inches in diameter with a gilt outer case, pierced and engraved with an English enamel, the bezel set with a diamond and a ruby, and it has a carillon of six bells. The watch plays a tune at each hour, and figures pass over a bridge, over a waterfall composed of twisted glass rods, which, in turning, give an appearance of flowing water.'

Another ingenious clock was made in the early seventeenth century
by the Reverend John Jones, Chancellor of Llandaff. He invented a
clock which was moved by air, this emanating from cylindrical
bellows. In the seventeenth century, too, the foundations of the
renowned clock craft at Llanrwst, North Wales, were laid. Watkin
Owen, a famed craftsman, was a member of a skilled family of
clockmakers.

By the eighteenth century clocks were usual in Welsh homes.
Clocks had a simple mechanism. They were set in long cases, which
were usually made by local carpenters. As with several other crafts,
clock-making tended to become established within a particular
family. The names of certain clockmakers were in themselves hallmarks of efficiency. Among the more renowned names were those
of Griffiths of Denbigh; Hughes of Caernarvon; Ingram of Abergavenny; Joyce of Denbighshire; Moseley of Swansea; Owen of
Llanrwst; Phillips of Haverfordwest; Tolemans of Caernarvon; Watkins of Monmouthshire; and the Winstanleys of Flint.

Some of the skill in clock-making was probably learnt in London,
where youths were apprenticed to the craft, sometimes by charitable organisations. A great number of clocks were, however, made in
Wales. 'I am satisfied they did not import their clocks', says Dr
Peate, 'but made them themselves with the help of carpenters who
made the cases, and the local foundries who supplied the weight.'
Initials inscribed on the clock weights suggest that they were made
to an express order of the clockmaker. Couplets from the works
of the early Welsh poets were sometimes engraved on brass dials.
Welshmen prided themselves on the fact that they were the creators
of clocks, not assemblers of parts, conveyed into the country by
the usual channels of trade. The pride with which the clockmakers
inscribed and numbered their clocks reflected well on their honest
workmanship and care. As time went on clockmakers in Wales
tended to become assemblers of parts, and repairers. Sometimes
parts were imported in their unfinished state. Toleman of Pwllheli
used to obtain the movements from one firm, and the dials from
another. He undertook the finishing of the brass movements, and
he engraved the dials. Weights were obtained from a local foundry,
and long cases were made by local carpenters.

Strong competition came from foreign clockmakers, who found refuge in Wales in the nineteenth century. Some Welshmen served as assistants and repairers to German and Polish clockmakers who settled in the new towns. The craft was fostered in the last decades of the nineteenth century at Llangollen, where Richard Hughes set up a factory for making watches. He employed a number of workmen from Coventry. His sons later took over the prosperous business.

In the twentieth century Welshmen made important contributions to the craft of clock-making. In the period 1905–7 the synchronome electrical master clock was presented by F. Hope-Jones. In 1916 Sir John Morris-Jones, Welsh scholar and professor at University College, Bangor, completed a master clock which worked three impulse dials the clock, which also worked on the synchronome principle, is now preserved in the National Museum of Wales.

8

Ceramics

"ONID OES AWDURDOD I'R CROCHENYDD AR Y PRIDDGIST, I WNEUTHUR O'R UN TELPYN PRIDD UN LLESTR I BARCH, AC ARALL I AMMARCH?" RHUFEINIAID 9 – 21

"HATH NOT THE POTTER POWER OVER THE CLAY, OF THE SAME LUMP TO MAKE ONE VESSEL UNTO HONOUR, AND ANOTHER UNTO DISHONOUR?" ROMANS 9 – 21

Gwenni Pottery Estd. 1610

◁ CROCHENYDD ⬦ DAVID JENKINS ⬦ POTTER ▷

POTTERY

Pottery, one of the world's oldest crafts, is practised widely in Wales. The craft potters perpetuate the old traditions and create functional domestic ware. Some artist-craftsmen, however, concentrate on making non-functional decorative objects.

The four basic techniques of pottery are practised. Potters shape clay entirely by hand, or by 'throwing' on a wheel. Another method is casting liquid clay in a mould, and yet another is that by which the potter presses the wet clay into a mould, either by hand or by machine. The pot is fired in a special prepared kiln. By the traditional method, the kiln is fuelled either by wood or coal. Modern kilns are, however, fuelled by oil, gas or electricity. The pot is then glazed, and returned to the kiln for a second session.

Many potters of today have studio potteries, usually in rural Wales, where visitors are welcome. These include:

Sansome Pottery, at Pontfadog, near Llangollen, who take pride in a variety of stone ware and terracotta pots for use in home and in garden. Here, the pots are hand-thrown from clay prepared on the premises. Visitors are able to see the craft in its various stages.

Taurus Crafts, The Old Pilot House, Bull Bay, Anglesey, is the successful venture of Michael and Ann Mumford. Michael was an engineer and Ann had studied art. She has developed a wide range of pottery, thrown on a wheel, stone pottery, coiled and pinched. It is made solely by hand. Some of her pinch pots are of outstanding design and workmanship.

Michael, with engineering experience behind him, developed a potter's wheel with a number of simple but ingenious accessories, which enable a range of pots to be turned out by someone of limited skill.

Taurus Crafts designed a modular range of pots so that a limited number of individual shapes can be used for a number of different finished articles. Thus, a simple beaker becomes a mug by the addition of a handle; two beakers, fastened together base to base, the two bottoms cut out and one end closed, make a flower vase. A storage jar with the addition of a spout and handle becomes a coffee pot. The lid is adapted from a standard saucer. The idea is not new, but the elements in the Bull Bay Pottery have been designed with such care, and the shapes are so simple and elegant, that they are individual and artistic.

Another successful venture is the creation of pottery replicas in various sizes with the old Parys Copper Mines tokens. The Parys pennies were made and circulated in the eighteenth century. It is estimated that nine million were minted. Some of these tokens are used to decorate pottery. Bigger ones are made into wall plaques, and the centres of large plates.

At the *Pottery, Penybont, Llandrindod Wells, Powys,* a wide range of work is undertaken. Household utensils are made in oxidised stoneware, soup bowls are made in pottery and sculptures are made in earthenware. Of special appeal are tin-glazed green plates which have a wax-resist pattern, with bud designs in the centre, painted in underglaze colours.

The John Hughes Pottery, Broadway, Pontypridd, is a gallery workshop. Well-known ceramic figures are made based on Welsh mythology and history and contemporary personalities.

The clay used in the potteries of South Wales is found in the main on the banks of rivers, where it has been carried by water, rendering it into an excellent constituency for the potter's wheel. At Raglan, Llantarnam and Ewenny, pottery of red and yellow colour is made. Ewenny was fortunately situated. The clay is of good quality and the coal pits are nearby. Neath, Swansea and Bridgend are good market centres. The Vale of Glamorgan demanded wares for the farm and dairy and the densely-populated industrial belt required household utensils. These Ewenny could provide by way of its three potteries.

At Buckley in North Wales potters found a ready market for their wares in the hill farms and in the industrial areas of the north-east. They specialised too, in the production of 'lead pots'. These were used in industries where white lead is extracted from pig iron. The earthenware pots, measuring about four inches deep and six inches in width, were used for holding the iron and acids.

The coarser clay at Buckley was used in brick work. The good yellow clay was glazed and made into fine firebricks. Such clay is plentiful. Sand firing materials and oxide of iron are mixed for the creating of firebricks. After puddling, the mixture is moulded into bricks, which are dried in the open before they are baked in kilns. Hand-made bricks, beautiful in themselves, and in their variety, can stand the test of several centuries' duration, as has been proved – and such bricks weather gracefully. Roofing tiles of clay and land drain pipes are also produced in the rural brickyards.

NANTGARW AND SWANSEA CHINA

Articles of both Nantgarw and of Swansea china are treasured collectors' pieces today.

Porcelain – true china – was for long the perquisite of the rich. Some of the finest china was made at Nantgarw, near Caerphilly, and at Swansea, during the nineteenth century. The work represented the enterprise of Englishmen. Nothing of a traditionally Welsh nature was incorporated in the making of the porcelain. Yet there was a very close association with Wales. It is pleasant to reflect, too, that Welsh men and Welsh women assisted in the creation of this remarkably beautiful china, and to realise that it was in the Principality that the china was made.

The hey-day of Nantgarw and of Swansea china was in the decade 1814–1824. The manufacture of porcelain was something of an innovation in Swansea, but earthenware potteries had flourished there since about 1770. The early factory at Swansea was associated with the name of George Hayman, and later with that of Lewis Llewellyn Dillwyn and of Lewis Weston Dillwyn.

In 1813 William Billingsley left the Royal Porcelain Works at Worcester, and arrived with his family at Nantgarw in the parish of Eglwysilian, Glamorgan. His choice of site for his pottery has been a subject of speculation; it is possible that secrecy concerning his past life or his enterprise may have affected his decision. In his favour was the nearness of the local coalfield, the proximity of a mill for grinding, and of the Glamorgan canal, which would enable him to transport his fragile wares at the minimum cost. He may at times have regretted that he had not settled in Bristol, where new material and skilled and semi-skilled labour were abundant. At Nantgarw he was a pioneer for no pottery had existed there before; skilled labour was non-existent, and markets were distant and dubious.

Assisted by Samuel Walker, his son-in-law, Billingsley set up at Nantgarw in 1815 two small firing kilns. Materials were obtained from Bristol. Financial support was given by William Weston Young. Difficulties at the Nantgarw pottery resulted in the removal of Billingsley and Walker to the Swansea pottery, but due to the continued financial support of William Weston Young, they were able to re-open the pottery at Nantgarw in 1817. There they remained until their removal to Coalport in 1819. Under the care of Young, the Nantgarw factory continued to operate until 1822. The factory passed into the hands of William Henry Pardoe in 1835.

The factory at Nantgarw experienced many vicissitudes. It has been estimated that in six years close on £4,000 was lost. The number of persons employed was small. At one time the workforce numbered 20, of whom 12 were children. Billingsley was 'a thin man of middle height, fair, with grey hair, but had no beard; he was a pleasant speaking man but very hot-tempered. He kept a horse-whip to thrash the boys and girls if they neglected their work.'

He and Walker must have worked unceasingly during their peak period of two and a half years at Nantgarw. Their success was great, bringing world renown to their china, but this success was dearly bought in effort as well as finance. Billingsley's avowed purpose at Nantgarw was to provide a soft paste porcelain which could hold its own alongside the old *pâte tendre* of Sèvres. How well he realised his ambition is apparent from an examination of the particularly fine specimens of Nantgarw china which have survived.

Unlike most workers in porcelain, those at Nantgarw neither stamped nor incised distinguishing marks on their porcelain. So fragile and so delicate to fire was the porcelain body which they manufactured, that Billingsley and Weston restricted the shapes of their vessels. They concentrated on shapes likely to stand firing successfully, and produced in the main dessert and tea services and plates. When they did create cabinet pieces, they were careful to avoid those which were disproportionately high in comparison to their width at the base. Consequently they did not make tall vases likely to collapse in the biscuit kiln, but instead they created a variety of candlesticks, pen trays, ink stands, tasses and pomade pots.

The Nantgarw porcelain possessed a coveted iridescence on its surface glaze. This was achieved after tremendous effort by an uncontrolled reaction during the firing process.

Much of the white china produced at Nantgarw was sent to London enamellers for decoration, but some of the finest specimens produced in Wales were decorated in the Principality.

Foremost among the decorators was Thomas Pardoe. From 1795 to 1802 he was the foremost decorator of pottery and porcelain at the Cambrian factory at Swansea. His versatility as a craftsman becomes evident when it is realised that he 'was also proficient in the skilled arts of staining, colouring, and etching of glass for churches and country mansions; he painted effectively too, on velvet-textured materials, for use on bell-pulls, covers and hangings'. Pardoe's output at the Cambrian factory at Swansea is altogether astonishing. He painted in monochrome and in rich natural colours. His subjects included birds and animals, flowers and landscapes, heraldic devices and portraits. He also introduced under-glazes and overglazes, and he painted earthenware as well as china.

Though he, too, was highly skilled in painting, Billingsley's time and energy were devoted at Nantgarw to the manufacture of porcelain. His work at Swansea had brought him into association with Pardoe, and the skill of the latter was enlisted for the decoration of Nantgarw china. There he painted his usual designs and landscapes which were of a topographical interest. His greatest contribution to the fine china of Nantgarw was the deep blue underglaze which he used for borders.

In his book, *Nantgarw Porcelain*, W. D. John pays tribute to the work of Thomas Pardoe:

'In considering Thomas Pardoe as a ceramic artist, it will generally be admitted that he was extraordinarily versatile, and that he could paint on either earthenware or porcelain almost everything that was required of him, from elaborate flower, fruit, bird and landscape compositions, to the simple geometrical drawings and lines of patterned borders; his underglaze blue colour, too, possesses a reasonable degree of purity and brilliance. Even more outstanding was his remarkable industry and the speed and execution of his work, for, without exception, he decorated more pottery and porcelain than any other well-known contemporary ceramic artist.

'Thomas Pardoe was an accomplished gilder, and did most of the gilding which accompanied the painting of flowers, birds, landscapes, borders, etc., varying this from broad bold bands and scrolls to delicate motifs and tracery works. At Nantgarw, in the closing days, to save the expense of gold, he used a chocolate coloured border with quite pleasing and satisfactory effect. His palette was not very extensive, but in Bristol and at Nantgarw it had the merit of containing a number of attractive and bright colours, including pink, pale yellow, and deep purple.'

9

Decorative Crafts

STAINED GLASS

Celtic Products of Prospect Place, Swansea. This small group of Swansea craftsmen is unique in Wales. The firm makes stained-glass windows. Demand for their work is such that the craftsmen are constantly at work assiduously to meet the demands of their order book, both for the home and foreign market. Hand-made Swansea windows are being fitted in the United States and Canada and South Africa.

The studio's chief designer is Mr Hubert Thomas. Speaking of the beautiful stained-glass windows made in Celtic Studios, he said: 'Real craftsmanship is very much in demand still. Bigger companies may be able to produce faster, but we pride ourselves on meticulous attention to detail.'

The firm specialises in ecclesiastical and secular stained-glass windows. Their work includes the use of architectural, and 'Dall de Verre' glass, glass appliqué and abstract colour glazing.

Wales has a rich tradition of stained glass. It is in recent years that the country has become aware of this. The researches of Dr Mostyn Lewis, recorded in his book *Stained Glass in North Wales up to 1850* (John Sherratt & Son Ltd, Altrincham) have done much to establish its value.

Most of the older stained glass has been preserved in North Wales. Various theories have been put forward to explain this – immunity from Puritan destruction in the seventeenth century, greater isolation, greater economic prosperity, etc.

Most of the old stained glass is found in North-East Wales, in churches and manor houses. The work is of a high standard. What is believed to be the oldest example that has survived is at Treuddyn in Flintshire. Some very fine work shows an affinity with ecclesiastical work in England, such as Winchester and York. Much of the mediaeval glass of North Wales dates from about the close of the fifteenth century. Stained glass at Gresford and at Llangyrnog date from this time. Work of the sixteenth century has been preserved at Llanrhaeadr and Dyserth. Much of the work of the period has the stamp of the individual craftsmen.

Much seventeenth-century work was armorial, showing a detailed knowledge of heraldry. Outstanding examples are at Mostyn Hall, Brynkialt, Llanerch Hall and Plas Newydd. Examples of painted armorial glass by the famed Francis Egerton of Birmingham (1757–1805) are to be seen at Marchwiel and St Asaph.

Outstanding among the glass painters of Wales was David Evans of Shrewsbury (1793–1862), a native of Llanllwchaiarn, near Newtown, Montgomeryshire. He was an apprentice of John Betton of Shrewsbury, and later became a partner in the well-known firm of Betton and Evans.

Evans revived the mediaeval technique of leaded pot metal. He used other media also. Silver stain and coloured enamel were introduced into his heraldic work. He used red enamel for fine detail.

Dr Mostyn Lewis pays tribute to David Evans as a colourist:

'His windows glow with the glory of brilliant colour, which is so well balanced as never to be garish, except in his last years when he lost his colour balance.'

Evans' drawings did not come up to the level of his colouring; but the defects in great measure are obliterated by the total effect achieved by rich colouring. Examples of his work are to be seen in Bangor Cathedral and Penrhyn Castle.

MINIATURE PAINTING

Jennifer Conway of Brecon is an artist who has established herself internationally. Her work is becoming well-known in exhibitions, such as those of the Royal Society of Painters, Sculptors and Engravers, and among collectors.

Her talent is far above the average. She paints professionally in a studio in her home in her native Brecon. Her husband, a keen naturalist, shares in her delight in her art. Her paintings of the Brecon Beacons are greatly admired. The Brecon Beacons National Park, one of the most beautiful in the British Isles, gives inspiration for much of her work.

Her miniature water colours show a variety of wild and garden flowers. Her world in miniature is painted delicately. The miniatures have been praised by lepidopterists and botanists for the accuracy of the work. She paints small insects on twigs and grasses, and butterflies resting on petals and on leaves. She seeks to paint the flowers as they grow, and critics feel that she achieves her purpose remarkably well. She includes small objects that belong to their naturalistic settings – small shells, feathers, fallen leaves. She paints, as she herself says, in her miniatures 'the miniature worlds which are within the world'.

Painting in miniature is the art of painting pictures on a very small scale. The miniature must be examined closely, or held in the hand, in order to appreciate fully the dainty and precise character of the craftsmanship. A miniature is often a small portrait. The genesis of miniature painting is to be found in the art of the illuminator as far back as the 18th Egyptian dynasty. It featured prominently in illuminated missals as long as illumination was a living art.

In the world of art, however, a miniature is an independent work. It has its own *raison d'être*. Hans Holbein was probably the earliest to practise the art. Miniatures came into special favour in Britain.

Nicholas Hilliard, Isaac Olwen and Samuel Cooper, were famed miniaturists of the sixteenth and seventeenth centuries. They favoured water colours. Later, oils were used. Miniatures in 'plumbago' or lead pencil had a great vogue. The early nineteenth century also had a number of fine workers in miniature, including Andrew Robertson Chalon and Sir W. Ross. In the early eighteenth century Rosalba Carriera greatly stimulated the art. Early miniatures were on vellum or card, but towards the end of the seventeenth century ivory was used for water colour. Many miniature pictures were executed in gouache and enamel pictures were used to embellish snuff boxes and similar articles. Miniature painting suffered with the coming of photography.

DRIED FLOWERS

Mrs Delia Squire Johnson of High Point, Llanfairpwll, Isle of Anglesey, creates pictures from flowers and leaves. Many of her pictures contain as many as 50 different flowers, leaves and grasses. Some of these are taken from her own garden. Others come from the countryside. She is fortunate in having close at hand the tremendous variety and quiet beauty of the flowers of the Isle of Anglesey.

The flower pictures which Mrs Johnson creates vary in size, from very small pictures which are 3½ inches square, to very large pictures measuring approximately 20 inches by 16 inches. The pictures are mounted and framed. The smaller frames are in metal, and the larger ones in wood. The pictures are bought by people from all over the world. She has won many prizes for her work, and has held very successful exhibitions in the National Eisteddfod of Wales.

This artist in flowers has a deep love for them. She says that one must choose carefully and never despoil. The flowers she uses for her pictures, she picks in full bloom. They are never picked at midday, and never gathered when wet. They are left for two months or more to dry and cure, pressed between layers of blotting paper or newspaper. She says: 'Experience will tell which flowers press the best.'

There is a tradition of preserving the flowers, leaves and grasses of summer in Wales, dating back to Victorian times, when the art was one of the accomplishments taught in seminaries for young ladies. Then, it was the custom to preserve them under glass globes.

Today, they are usually mounted and placed in picture frames. It is a delightful craft which has direct association with the country-side.

Flowers gathered in high summer were arranged with leaves gathered in autumn to form fine collage pictures. Special presses were available for drying. Thick stalks were discarded and flowers, leaves and seeds were dried separately. The petals of roses were peeled off the main stalk and pressed. Then they were re-assembled as a flower. Certain flowers were split down the middle, and a half flower was then pressed. Deeper tones were achieved by laying a second row of petals over the first. The stalks of other flowers were often introduced when delicate effects were needed. The flowers and stalks placed between blotting paper were subjected to heavy pressure. Heavy books were laid to rest over them. An alternative method was to place them under a carpet.

A Victorian and Edwardian custom (which has been revived) was the making of personal greeting cards decorated with pictures made by leaf skeletons. All vegetable matter was removed by boiling or by immersion in soda and water. The skeleton was then dried – and sometimes dyed. Flowers of summer were dried for winter use by hanging them up. Some were covered with layers of borax. This made them more brittle, but it had the advantage of preserving, and even heightening their colour. Such flowers and leaves were often arranged artistically on a base of clay, the stalks being inserted into it.

MUSICAL INSTRUMENTS

Robin Haddaway, of Llanio Road, Tregaron, Ceredigion, makes musical instruments for professional musicians. He concentrates on instruments that were played from about 1550–1700 in Britain and in Europe generally.

He makes plucked and bowed instruments of this period. His special interest is in wire-string plucked instruments, such as zithers, and some of the bowed instruments of the sixteenth century, viols and lyra de gamba, and early members of the violin family. Occasionally he makes telves and fradles. He has made a Welsh *crwth* and hopes to make a harp. He takes special interest in instruments which originated in Italy in the sixteenth to the eighteenth centuries, and others invented in Britain in the late sixteenth century.

He obtains all his wood from the East where the rainfall is small. Parts of the instruments are made with hard woods from the tropics. Wood from Switzerland is used for sound boards.

Robin Haddaway is a lone craftsman. Such is the demand for his work that he hopes to get an assistant.

His range is small but highly specialised. Most of his work is sold abroad. He travels abroad much in order to obtain first-hand knowledge of the traditional techniques employed in making the instruments.

LACE-MAKING

Mrs Marjorie Carter, an expert in the making of pillow lace, is influential in the revival and practice of the craft. Further, she is Secretary of the *Lace Society, Wales*.

There is revived interest in the making of pillow lace. Courses have been arranged at Missenden Abbey in Buckinghamshire, Maryland, the Bedfordshire Adult College at Woburn, the Craft College at West Dean in Sussex, among other places.

Mrs Carter began to teach lace-making to adults during the last war. At that time, second-hand materials were used to make improvised pillows. Threads and bobbins, such as were available, were used. Since then she has taught pillow lace continuously. A strong proportion of her students have been adults, but she has also taught young girls in schools. There has been great satisfaction in seeing the subject included in school-leaving certificates.

Do modern girls appreciate this craft which requires patience, and in the early stages, perseverance? Mrs. Carter answers emphatically in the affirmative. The girls get rich satisfaction from producing something beautiful, and they realise that even now it is still an unusual craft for very young people. The teacher finds inspiration in the knowledge that she is introducing the very young to the art, and that they, in turn, will be able to pass it on to another generation.

Several types of pillow lace exist, and fortunately they are in circulation again. A beginner usually starts with torchon; the geometrical designs are reasonably easy for them. A pupil advances to Cluny and to Bedford-Maltese patterns, with their plaits and picots and 'leaves'. She graduates to the very beautiful Buckinghamshire lace, and then to a variety of types from the Eastern European countries. Finally, there is devoted effort in the creation of Honiton lace, which has been revived, and which was greatly treasured in Victorian days.

Most of the pillow lace is made for personal satisfaction. Its creators do not expect to make a living from it. They experience joy in seeing their own and others' efforts rewarded by making some-thing lovely, a joy that cannot be expressed in mere words. They realise that they are indeed making heirlooms for the future. There are a few people, however, who are prepared to make it for sale.

Lace-making must be regarded as an individual and personal craft. Crochet work, which was very prevalent in the first three decades of the century, also contributed to the beauty and elegance of homes, and also of ecclesiastical edifices.

The Lace Society, Wales, has in recent years done valuable work in reviving the craft of pillow lace. This form of lace has been undergoing a very considerable revival. The spread of interest began after the last war, starting slowly and gradually gaining momentum. Classes have been formed all over the country. Week-end courses have been arranged in places where the making of pillow lace is traditional, and in Colleges of Further Education.

The Lace Society has gone on from strength to strength from modest beginnings in 1968. Members are now counted in hundreds, and newcomers are joining the ranks all the time.

FEATHER-CRAFT

The poultry yard of a mixed farm in Wales is usually the house-wife's domain. For long, feathers were treasured as filling for beds. Whatever the debit side of the matter, many country folk remain loyal to their preference for feather beds. The farmer's wife may still obtain prices which are good, if not high, for white goose down, and for poultry feathers.

By a paradox, poultry *dressed* for market is undressed – i.e. the birds are deprived of their feathers. A farmer's wife usually sees to her own requirements first. She will make or replenish feather beds and pillows for her own household. She will make cushions for old oak chairs, and will make a long bolster-shaped cushion for the *sciw*, or draught-excluding settle, which is given an honoured place in the farm kitchen. She will sell surplus feathers to dealers who come around the farms, or who are established in the market towns.

The lore of preserving feathers has survived. When the poultry are being prepared for table, all fowl feathers are removed. The clean feathers are fastened into a bag of old linen and are placed in a moderately heated oven. Alternatively the feathers are placed in an old linen sheet, and hung up to dry near the fireplace. When thoroughly dry they are poured into a bed or pillow tick, which has been coated on the inside with beeswax or soap to prevent the feathers working their way out. The pillow is then placed near gentle heat to swell up.

Poultry feathers, white and coloured, are now used indiscriminately. At one time they were graded carefully. Best beds were of goose down. Pillows of swansdown were greatly valued. The wing feathers of a goose are still valued as dust removers. Goose quills are also used in the manufacture of paint brushes.

The craft of preserving feathers remains a hearthside craft, serving essentially household needs. Old traditions have a way of seeping into modern life. Even today, there are few who would fill a pillow tick with feathers of birds of flight – pigeon, pheasant, wild duck. Peacock feathers are regarded as unlucky. Racial tradition maintains that feathers from birds of flight banish sleep.

PERFUME

The fragrant perfumes collected and preserved by the *Cistercian monks on Caldey Island* are now internationally known.

The island, which lies off the rugged coast of Wales in Pembrokeshire, Dyfed, has been the home of monks for 14 centuries. Monks of the Cistercian order are there today; they cultivate the island of 300 acres, continuing a tradition begun by a Celtic settlement in the sixth century. An atmosphere of peace and of unhurried care prevails, and it is in this setting that the Cistercians of Caldey have developed their perfumery. Hand-made, hand-bottled, and hand-packed, they give to their craft the individual attention which is so alien to the competitive, commercial world. Knowledge of perfumery has been obtained in the best schools. Leading authorities are constantly consulted, and only the purest oils are used.

The fragrances that are collected and preserved are distilled from the wild flowers which grow in abundance on the island. The perfumes are evocative of a way of life, of a tranquillity, and of an environment which contrasts completely with the world of materialism, mechanisation and noise.

Gorse grows plentifully on the island. The perfume Island Gorse has a woody fragrance, heightened by a spicy tang. Island Bouquet captures the fragrance of the wild flowers growing on the island. Each perfume has its matching cologne. Toilet soaps and hand lotions are made from the best base oils; the perfume compounds are made by the monks. Potpourri is made from a mixture of flowers, gums and resins, developed by the monks over many years. More than 20 different kinds of flowers are put into the potpourri, and more than a dozen gums and resins.

Ingenuity is shown in the creation of pomanders. They contain 20 different kinds of flowers, including cornflowers, marigolds and peonies, and many others. The addition of rare woods and resins such as Benzoim Siam, Yellow Sandalwood, Olibanum and Tonka Beans. A unique and sweet-smelling blend results. Animal pomanders representing dogs, elephants, hedgehogs and owls are hand-made. Seashell pomanders represent colourful marine life and fish. The Tudor Ball of Caldey is decorated in colour. Pomanders were popular in Tudor times. The Tudor dynasty had close links with Pembrokeshire.

Perfumery deals with the preparation of fragrant smelling-substances used for toilet purposes. The work consists of extracting the odours of plants; leaves and flower buds are the chief sources of supply. The odours or perfumes of plants are isolated by different means; they are rendered applicable for use and are then absorbed in various materials such as fats, grease, oil, spirit and soaps, and also inert materials such as starch and talc.

The process of extracting the odours is intricate. It can take the form of distillation by enfleurage, by maceration, and by expression. In distillation, flower petals, buds, and sometimes the seeds of plants are placed in a still with water. The mixture is distilled; the otto rises with the steam. It is taken to a receiver where it forms a layer on the surface of the water. It is then separated by decantation, or it is siphoned off. The amount of perfume yielded by distillation varies considerably, depending upon the plants used. The ottos become soluble in alcohol, and they are also absorbed by fixed oils and by fats.

The method of enfleurage entails the use of wooden frames, two or three inches deep, and fitted with glass bases. The latter are covered with a layer of grease, and the flower buds are sprinkled over them. The frames are put to rest over one another. They are left for a day or two, and the flowers are then removed, and another layer of flowers is laid on. The process is continued as long as that particular flower is in bloom. The grease is then scraped off, and used to perfume soap, etc. Pure olive oil is used sometimes to saturate the flower buds.

By the method of maceration leaves or buds are saturated in a particular medium, e.g. spirits. Dry powder, such as starch moistened with alcohol, is an alternative medium.

JEWELLERY

Craftsmen and women specialising in the making of jewellery find ready co-operation from companies that make jewellery, such as *Ammonite Ltd, of Llandow, Cowbridge*. The equipment required is relatively simple. It includes snub-nosed pliers, abrasive stick, and adhesive, and plasticine or sand hay. Mountings, both drop and flat, and also claw, can be bought. Tumble-polished stones can also be bought. Cast mountings are supplied with silver and gold finish.

Rocks that date back for millennia are treasured today by craftsmen for their beauty and colouring. Collectors gather them with infinite patience. They polish them and bring out their rich colourings. There is a wide variety of stones from which they can select: amber, with its lights varying from yellow to red; agate, golden grey; amethyst, violet and chalk white; bloodstone, heliotrope; chalcedony, a translucent blue-grey and fawn; carnelian, a flashing red; cairngorm, a clear golden brown; citrine, a chalk white with tinges of yellow; flint, grey to black; fluorspar, with pastel coloured crystals, granite, pink grey flecked with black; jasper, green, yellow and terracotta.

The stones have their own natural beauty acquired through the centuries in sea and river. Hidden beauty is revealed by polishing, either by hand, or with a tumbler polisher.

Stones are classified according to their hardness. Hand polishing is necessary for the softer stones.

For jewellery, the stones are chosen according to their shape. Those stones which are shaped, domed and rounded, are termed cabochon. A faceted stone is one which has been ground so as to have a flat surface. The term baroque is used when a stone is left in its natural irregular shape. Stones are mounted on metal fittings and made into rings, pendants, bracelets and ear-rings.

GLASS-BLOWING

Enzo and Wendy Speranza of Saundersfoot have business acumen as well as artistic ability. In only a matter of months they established themselves in the country, and broke into the export market. They are fortunately placed for the tourist trade, and are glad of the respite of winter months to replenish their warehouses, which are literally bare at the close of summer. More skilled staff will be enlisted.

Enzo Speranza has wide experience in his craft. He learnt his skill as a glass blower in his native Italy. After working in several European countries, he set up a small workshop – Avondale Glass, near Saundersfoot.

Free of competition and with reduced overheads, and with a highly demanding market, the Speranzas face the future hopefully.

Their stock is of a highly valued character. They specialise in ash trays, vases and paperweights. There is a steady demand for the paperweights in the United States, and exports also go to Canada and Europe generally.

MINIATURES

Mr Roger Jones, director of *Acorn Workshops, Milton, Pembroke*, has a workshop which specialises in wooden products. He has had considerable success as a maker of toys. In the competitive world of commerce, his problem is to keep his craft miniature in scale. There is an ever increasing demand for the range of unusual musical instruments which he is creating.

He has designed a 24-stringed psaltery which was indigenous in the Middle East, and also an African thumb piano. Particularly popular is his miniature version of the Welsh harp.

Mr Jones holds firm views about his workshop. He is determined to employ craftsmen. He does not want the workshops to become mere production-lines. He says: 'I prefer to be a craftsman rather than a businessman. I prefer the sawdust of the workshop to an office chair.'

Daniel D. Jenkins and Son of Woodlands, Cross Hands, Llanelli, Dyfed, is a small firm, but with a big output.

Each year it uses many tons of timber to make a wide range of products in miniature – replicas of Welsh furniture, milking stools, sailing ships. Of special appeal is a Welsh harp, just nine inches high, and a three-quarter full size Welsh dresser.

The firm makes spinning wheels in four sizes, including a full-size working model. The craftsmen concentrate on making models and furniture which are traditionally Welsh, including rocking chairs, chests of drawers and cradles. A speciality is a coal train containing real anthracite coal.

CANDLES

Candles today are not restricted to functional use: they can be moulded, carved or dipped. They are made in many colours and in intricate and individual designs. Beautiful candle holders are made in pottery.

Candles in the Rain, The Old Smithy, Nantglyn, Denbigh, Clwyd. Hand-made candles in individual shapes, and in many colours are a speciality.

Candles are made by melting down suitable fat in hot water, over a very low heat. Colouring is added with a grease-based dye, and sometimes a dye of powder paints.

The craftsman gives much thought to his moulds, bearing in mind that he has to get the candle out when set. Shapes and depths are various. Wicks made of special wick string are inserted, and held in place while the wax sets. Layers of colour are introduced. When the first layer has almost set, the next layer is poured on, the timing being important to ensure that each layer of wax is bonded properly.

The lighting of the home has been an important matter in the life of civilised man. The making of candles was formerly a prominent occupation in the home of nobleman and peasant alike.

The Romans used candles of bees-wax, and it is probable that the early Britons were familiar with the sight of these set alight in Roman shrines. It was not until the thirteenth century that they came to be used in the homes of noblemen in Europe. Later they feature as expensive items in the accounts of lords and monasteries, for candles up to the number of several thousand were needed to illuminate the great halls of mediaeval architecture. With the Renaissance came the rise of guilds of candle makers, by whom the size and ingredients of candles were regulated.

The commonalty at large, by trial and error, made candles for

W.C.—K

its own particular needs. Employing materials to hand, men made candles by various methods.

Most familiar to the peasant was the rush light. Its soft and constant illumination is still known in the remoter areas of West and North Wales. A fine day in mid-summer was set aside for the gathering of rushes. These were stripped of their peel. One length of peel was left as a hinge for the soft resilient pith. Oddments of fat were heated in a shallow pan kept for the purpose. The rushes were soaked in the grease and then set aside to cool. The rush light remained supple even when the fat had hardened. Because of this a holder was essential. Rush-light holders called out the ingenuity and the artistry of the country craftsman. Holders were usually of iron fitted into a stone or wooden base. They were sometimes ornamented. The socket demanded skill; sometimes it was fitted with a wire spring clip, sheathed with tin. The most usual type of rush-light holder was a simple nipper device fitted with a light spring and weighted by the candle. Hanging holders were fitted with racks. The height of the candle could thus be adjusted within an iron lantern. These hanging holders were usual in churches.

Rush candles were another device. They burned more quickly than rush lights. A day was set aside for their making. The smell of the grease was obnoxious. The outer rushes were peeled, with the exception of two strips of skin left on either side of the pith to support it, and to delay too hasty burning. The rush was dipped into melted fat and left to dry. When the tallow had hardened, the process was repeated. After several operations the necessary thickness was acquired. The porous rush piths were considered superior to candlewick.

Fat saved from cooking was used. Beef fat was considered superior for the purpose. Some thrifty peasants used to advantage the waxen berries of the bayberry tree. The grey-blue fruit was boiled in shallow pans. The wax was culled from the top of the liquid. The dark colour of the wax not being acceptable, it was refined. It appeared on the wicks in an attractive green colour. The extra work in obtaining this was considered well worth the effort, for rush wicks coated with it were hard and non-greasy and remained solid in warm atmospheres.

Tallow candles, fitted with candlewick, were also used. These were also made in farm houses and cottages. Sufficient for a season, or for a year, was made, for the work involved upheaval in the home, and the smell of the melting grease was not pleasant. As with the rush candles, tallow was melted in a pan or kettle. A supply of candle poles or rattans was part of the household equipment. These were hung parallel between two supports. A series of smooth sticks were hung between the rods. Strips of cotton, hemp or tow, were used for candlewicking. These strips were twice the length of the candle. A strip was twisted round and suspended from the candle rod in such a way that the ends were brought together at the top. A double twist was made ensuring a slow-burning wick. A series of wicks was hung by loops from the candle rod. Care was taken that the wicks did not touch each other in the process of being coated.

When the wicks had been prepared, the cauldron of boiling tallow was removed from the fire. Tallow floated at the top, but water lay at the bottom. Consequently, these candles were sometimes referred to as water-candles, *cannwyll y dwfr*.

The work was often done in the open. The candle rods were taken from the horizontal bars and were each dipped in the fat. When all the wicks on each of the rods had been dipped, the process was repeated. It was tedious work, but at last the candles were of a thickness required to fit into the holders. From time to time the housewife poured boiling water into the cauldron, so that the tallow rose to the top and the candles could be immersed in it.

Moulds of pewter and of tin were later used. This meant an economy of time and of material. The housewife could now make a half-dozen or a dozen candles at a time. The mould was made in such a way that a wick could be inserted. When this was in place, tallow was poured around it, and kept secure in the mould until cool.

Candle making was not a welcome job, and women patronised itinerant candlemakers who travelled the Welsh countryside bringing great moulds for making two dozen candles in one process. Tallow was a precious commodity. Oddments left over from candle making were melted in a special iron cauldron. Frequent applications of the melted fat made boots and leggings of cow-hide pliant and weatherproof.

Candle holders were made in different styles and materials. The Romans had candle holders made from pottery. Saucers to hold the melting grease were introduced in the Middle Ages, especially for use in churches. Candle holders were fitted with vertical holders, and thus became candlesticks. Made in brass, pewter, or tin, candlesticks became features of the Welsh house in the eighteenth century. Devices were fitted to raise the candle as it burned. Snuffers, complete with trays, were additional accessories.

The actual process of candle-dipping was obnoxious but it had its pleasant side. A good-humoured peasantry sought to make good out of evil. Sir John Rhys in *Celtic Folk Lore, Welsh and Manx* records meeting a Robert Hughes who told him of the customs associated with candle-dipping:

> 'Story-telling was kept alive in the parish of Llanaelhaearn . . . by the institution known there as the *pilnos*, or peeling night, when the neighbours met in one another's houses to spend the long winter evenings dressing hemp and carding wool, though I guess that a *pilnos* was originally the night when people met to *peel* rushes for rush-lights.'

Hugh Evans, the author of *The Gorse Glen*, tells of his own experiences in peeling rushes:

> 'At one time, I believe, rush peeling was made an occasion for going from house to house, and there used to be a *noswaith bilo* – a peeling night – but that was before my time . . . Although I cannot remember a *noswaith bilo* I have peeled rushes scores of times, and thousands of rush lights were burned in my home and the other homes in Cwm Eithin during those years. It was interesting work enough, once you had learnt to do it without cutting your fingers, or breaking the pith of the rush. The peel will cut your finger to the bone if you are not careful. The process was this: you cut the points of the rushes, and then began to peel from the stem, leaving a strip about one sixteenth of an inch wide all along the pith to support and stiffen it. This done, the peeled rush would be steeped in hot fat on the frying pan, when the rush light would soon be ready for use. The holder in which they were kept was called a *dil*, and enough rush lights would be made at one time to fill the *dils*. When the rush was lit, it had to be moved every few minutes, as it burnt down to the holder unless you were holding it in the hand to read by.'

FINE BOOKBINDING

At the *Old Court, Caerwys, Mold, Mr Tom Lloyd Roberts* has a unique bookbinding service, specialising in old style binding and restoration. Fine modern bindings are made there by Paul Delrue, a highly-qualified artist-craftsman. He has the rare distinction of being able to do every kind of bookbinding, from restoration and traditional bindings to modern craft binding. He does all stages of bookbinding himself, without being part of a team as is the case in most binderies today.

Mr Roberts has himself a fine collection of beautifully bound books. Among the more remarkable are exquisite examples of Paul Delrue's work.

Three books, *Parrots in Captivity*, were specially bound at Old Court Bindery, Caerwys by Paul Delrue. In each case, the binding depicts in full colour one of the species dealt with in the books. The entire work is done with onlaid leathers. The three books stand up together with an additional design of leathered onlays which continues across all three books so that they form one design.

The Visitors Book at Old Court House was specially designed and bound at Old Court Bindery by Paul Delrue in 1976. The front cover has a design in onlaid leathers which reproduces the coat of arms of Tom Lloyd Roberts; the back cover has an onlaid design depicting the Mostyn Silver Harp, the ancient accolade of the early Welsh Eisteddfodau, which was last awarded in 1568 when William Mostyn organised the Eisteddfod, commissioned by Elizabeth I from his Court House (now Old Court Bindery, Caerwys).

Another book which has a fine modern binding and which is in the collection of Mr Roberts is a children's book of the late Victorian period, entitled *Young England's Nursery Rhymes*. The entire work is done in onlaid leathers using a technique of combining the two sides of the skins of leather to achieve depth and tone. No colouring of any kind was introduced. All has been achieved with the use of leather alone, even the blush on the boy's cheeks!

A fine binding done in traditional style has been used by Paul Delrue for work at Old Court Bindery. The book *Views of North and South Wales by Sir C. R. Colt Hoare* (1875) is bound in oasis morocco. It is richly tooled in gold leaf.

A book entitled *Elgar* is another in the private collection of Tom Lloyd Roberts which shows the work of Paul Delrue. This book was bound in 1976. The technique is unusual. The craftsman first made a landscape in leathers, using a mixture of the finished skins and the flesh side of the skin. The landscape has the appearance of the

Malvern Hills. He introduced no paint; he used leathers only. From this landscape he cut out the letters ELGAR and used them as onlaid leathers on to the book which he had bound in green oasis morocco. The 'leathered onlays' are part of Paul Delrue's style; he introduces them into his bindings whenever possible.

⊸ IO ⊂

Conclusion

THE CLOGMAKER

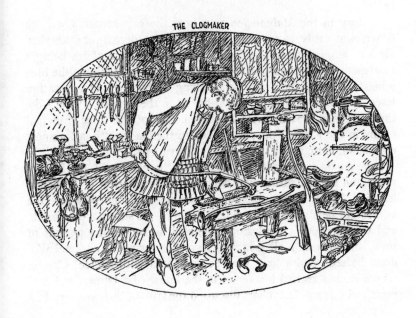

The future of the crafts in Wales is a constant preoccupation. No plea is put forward for their picturesque survival as a relic of a more leisurely past: their ethnological value is fully accredited. Wales is indeed fortunate in her Welsh Folk Museum at St Fagan's, Cardiff. It preserves in a living and inspiring way the rich folk culture of Wales, and many of the traditional crafts are practised there today by skilled craftsmen. The crafts of Wales have a meaning for the present and for the future. Their survival as living factors in the national life, must, of necessity, depend on the policy of the central government, and also on local influence which, in itself, demands things useful and beautiful.

Many of the crafts flourished when village life was self-sufficing;
several were adjuncts of husbandry. Some derive from the time
when the craftsman was himself a producer of food – witness the
coracle-maker of pre-Roman days, who was himself a fisherman.

The cultural significance of the crafts in Wales is acknowledged.
It was not the scholar, nor the bard, nor the ecclesiastic, who was
honoured most in the Court of King Arthur, *but he who plied his
craft.*

A story in the *Mabinogion* tells how the gate-keeper, Gwrnach
Gawr, was tardy in opening the gate to one of Arthur's Knights.
Sir Kay alone entered the Court, and this in virtue of his being a
craftsman, a burnisher of swords. He is described as taking 'the blue
whetstone under the armpit and asking "Which would you rather
have – the blue polish, or the white?" ' In the days of Hywel Dda,
the craftsman was likewise honoured. One of the three principal
chairs in the King's Court was given to the blacksmith, a foremost
craftsman, in that he was the maker of weapons.

Humanistic influences prevailed with the coming of the Renaissance and craftsmanship was depressed in the interest of academic
learning. Wales is an outstanding example of a country where the
two forces persisted side by side. The forge, the shoemaker's bench,
and the carpenter's workshop have each in succeeding periods of
time, and in nearly all localities formed a forum of national wisdom. Indeed, Wales may well be compared with ancient Greece,
where Homer recited his verses in the house of a tanner, and Soc-
rates and other philosophers discussed the laws of their country in a
craftsman's shop.

The scene in a Welsh country workshop in the late nineteenth
century has been described by the eminent philosopher, Sir Henry
Jones, when he wrote of his humble home in the Llangerniw in his
fascinating biography, *Old Memories.*

'I left school when I was 12½ years old, and put on my little
shoemaker's apron, and a new and most happy page of my life
was opened. There are few, if any, pleasanter scenes in the world
than those presented by the little workshops of the country shoemaker and tailor. There, master and man are working side by
side, talking freely with one another about anything and everything; for they sit quite near each other, and the strain of the
work is not so heavy and constant as to prevent either conver-

sation or singing. Not that the talk was not interrupted, or that the songs were ever sung right through. . . .

'Then there were discussions and debates and the village news had to go round, and my father was always crammed full of mischievous fun and anecdotes.

'The discussions and debates were rarely political, and never religious, but some of them would interest and occupy the mind of the workshop on and off for days. Above all, there was story-telling, and tales of the experiences of other days; and the chief of the story-tellers was my father. . . .

'Knowing the joys of the workshop as I did, I think it no wonder that I insisted on being a shoe-maker. . . . I knew in that decisive way which we call "feeling" that if I made shoes, I could hear and share in what was going on in the workshop; and I could sit side by side with my father, whose favourite I was, and whom I adored.'

Elsewhere the craftsman's workshop was often the scene of spirited political and religious debate. The craftsman himself was in many instances identified with the politician, the preacher, and the poet, the richness of the work of his hand finding its material comple-ment in the spiritual insight and aesthetic power of his mind. Individuality was the key-note of life. The skilled craftsman found sound satisfaction in his work, and he gave satisfaction to those for whom he worked. That the monetary payment for the work was low is not denied. Sound payment for sound work is a worthy maxim; then there is the philosophy that in the present century too much emphasis has been placed on payments, and too little on good work. Mass-production and mass-thought have doubtless im-poverished our national life. Wales may well give careful con-sideration to the policy of fostering traditional crafts alongside industrial development.

Crafts were at their most flourishing when practised among com-munities which were essentially local. The craftsman supplied a local need. Materials were obtained locally. The raw materials were fashioned near to the place where they were to be used. This policy makes one question, in the midst of the present-day commercial trading and transport system, whether this is the truest form of economy for our country.

The future of the crafts is largely bound up with the resuscitation of the Welsh countryside. Those communities which fostered the traditional crafts were largely self-supporting. Following on the changes which came with the Industrial Revolution, many of these areas became adjuncts to an alien town. Some of the ill-effects which followed were reduced by economic insight and sound planning. The rehabilitation of Welsh areas has won general approval. The swing of the pendulum is in many ways away from urban life. The virtues of rural life are being re-assessed. Problems of housing, sanitation, electricity, transport, etc., will have to be grappled with. Even so, more and more, the opportunities for individual effort and for personal responsibility are being investigated. Political economists stress the importance of re-populating whole belts of the Welsh countryside. They see in such a policy a substantial increase in the nation's food production. Such a policy would also work to the advantage of many small towns whose prosperity is bound up with that of the countryside. Settlement in the rural villages will bring blessings to the newcomers, and will also provide craftsmen with a direct market for their goods.

There was a democratic tradition in the Welsh village in the past. Farming was essentially the pivot of rural life. Directly or indirectly, all the people of the village were linked with the land. A social hierarchy did exist, but the squire, the parson, or the well-to-do farmer, though each given his mead of due respect, was not fundamentally regarded as superior. There was a racial consciousness, silent but strong. Likewise, there was a strong, if unexpressed spirit of commonwealth and of harmonious co-operation for the common good. If a man did not regard good workmanship as a sound working ideal, he was obviously a weak link in the community, and his neighbours did not hesitate to tell him so.

The spirit of co-operation has in it several distinct virtues. At intervals, usually in time of distress, it comes to the fore, inspiring action which is good. This spirit has persisted in farming communities, and among craftsmen. Its preservation is important.

The general migration from urban districts back to the country has in the past three to four decades developed along national lines. Herein lies the possibility of a natural and healthy revival of the crafts. Their progress and continued prosperity will, of necessity, depend on many other factors. One of the foremost of these will be the power of the crafts to adapt themselves to the needs of generations living at a faster rate than heretofore. Systems of barter and forms of the domestic system will have to conform with more usual forms of trading. Craftsmen are traditionally poor business-men, but economic forces as well as human organisations are already working to their good.

The emphasis on the 'back to the land' policy, and the develop-ment of agriculture, rank among the more powerful of forces assist-ing craftsmanship. The craftsman has ever been the ally of the farmer. In the midst of mechanised farming schemes, care will have to be taken that the craftsman does not become a mere repairer. He must ply his craft and develop it to serve the needs of the present and future generations.

Since the end of World War I policies of afforestation have had far-reaching effects on Wales. As the woodland crafts form the basis of many others in Wales, increased interest in forestry must inevit-ably give a strong fillip to craftsmanship. In the past, destruction of our forests has proved to be a national loss. Wisely-planned afforestation may help to counteract the evil. Timber shortage has sent up prices. The wise use of timber and of coppice wood by craftsmen working by hand, or using machinery on a small scale, may well prove a national investment, yielding worthy dividends.

Wales must play her part in facing realistically the scarcity of essential materials, and the need to create commodities; she must assist too in overcoming the monetary shortage which affects all commercial life. With advantage to herself and to her neighbours she must make full use of her resources. Her crafts can most assuredly assist her to material prosperity and to the revival of a balanced and happy society.

Index